TWIN FLAMES AND SOUL MATES

How to Find, Create, and Sustain Awakened Relationships

LUNA AND SOL

Copyright

Twin Flames and Soul Mates: How to Find, Create, and Sustain Awakened Relationships

Copyright © Aletheia Luna and Mateo Sol, 2019

All rights reserved. No part of this book may be reproduced or transmitted in any form or by any means, electronic or mechanical, including photocopying, recording, or by any information storage and retrieval system, without permission in writing by the authors.

The information contained in this book is intended to be educational and not for diagnosis, prescription, or treatment of any health disorder whatsoever. This information should not replace consultation with a competent healthcare professional. The authors are in no way liable for any misuse of the material.

All names and identifying details have been changed to protect the privacy of the individuals quoted in this book. Some first-hand accounts have been edited and re-worded for the sake of clarity.

Let there be spaces in your togetherness,

And let the winds of the heavens dance between you.

Love one another but make not a bond of love:

Let it rather be a moving sea between the shores of your souls.

Fill each other's cup but drink not from one cup.

Give one another of your bread but eat not from the same loaf.

Sing and dance together and be joyous, but let each one of you be alone,

Even as the strings of a lute are alone though they quiver with the same music.

Give your hearts, but not into each other's keeping.

For only the hand of Life can contain your hearts.

And stand together, yet not too near together:

For the pillars of the temple stand apart,

And the oak tree and the cypress grow not

in each other's shadow.

– Kahlil Gibran

For the lovers out there, the dreamers, the souls who are destined to make huge waves of change in this fragmented world: *this is for you.* May you be guided and supported. May you realize that you are a force of nature in a fleshly form. Together, you are what this world needs to evolve and awaken.

For the Divine forces that brought Luna and Sol together, thank you a million times over. Words fail to express our gratitude.

Table of Contents

Introduction 1

Chapter 1: Love and the Spiritual Awakening Process....... 7

Chapter 2: What is a Soul Mate? 12

Chapter 3: What is a Twin Flame?..................................... 27

Chapter 4: The Story of Luna and Sol 50

Chapter 5: How to Find Your Soul Mate and
Twin Flame 63

Chapter 6: Harmful Myths About Twin Flame and
Soul Mate Relationships 89

Chapter 7: The Five Levels of Relationships 107

Chapter 8: Are You in a Healthy Relationship?............. 116

Chapter 9: What to Do When Your Relationship
Falls Apart 148

Chapter 10: The Shadow Side of Seeking Love............. 173

Chapter 11: How to Use Your Relationship as a
Spiritual Catalyst 200

What Next? (Concluding Thoughts) 244

Appendix 1: Q&A.. 246

Appendix 2: Soul Mate Test 257

Appendix 3: Twin Flame Test 263

References 270

Bibliography.. 274

About the Authors... 276

Other Books by the Authors............................ 277

Introduction

This is a book about love: deep love, intense love, timeless love, transcendental love. It's also a book about the shadows of love, where love can go haywire, and how to find the true love that you seek.

Soul mate and twin flame love is an ancient concept. We see it in the dance between Shiva and Shakti, the union of the Horned God and Mother Goddess in old earth religions, the passion of Osiris and Isis, and the mystical symbiosis of Jesus and Mary Magdalene.

But while ancient and timeless, at no point in the history of civilization has there ever been as *intense* and *passionate* an interest in spiritual relationships as there is right now.

We have reached a critical point in our evolution as a species. Most of us are living in amazing times full of knowledge, science, technology, and material wealth. No other generation in the past has ever experienced this richness. But, the tragic reality is that most of us live in a profound level of spiritual poverty that has never been experienced or known since the dawn of humanity. Our eep us completely indoors. We move from our our cars, and our offices, and then back again, maybe with stops in the gym or the mall along the way. Our earth is buried by asphalt and our city lights hide the stars and planets.

Because of this disconnection from nature and the Divine, most of us end up pursuing empty materialistic goals that deepen our sense of loneliness and meaninglessness. We become cogs in the machine of society and spend our days laboring in jobs and roles that desecrate our souls. Yes, we may be outwardly expanding at unprecedented rates, but that comes at the expense of our profound inner impoverishment, confusion and alienation from each other.

What is the solution to the destruction of our beautiful planet and the gnawing existential emptiness growing in the hearts and minds of people worldwide? We believe the answer, in part, lies in the tremendous power of soul mate and twin flame relationships.

As the institution of traditional marriage and materialistic comfort-seeking relationships crumbles with a rise in divorce rates, our world, our very souls, are demanding something more. We are no longer satisfied with relationships of convenience, relationships that only satisfy our physical and emotional needs. We need relationships that nourish the soul, relationships that commit to deep spiritual evolution and transformation.

While soul mate and twin flame relationships are ancient, they are also new to the human experience. We don't yet have any social rules, conventions, or structures to help us navigate through such complex and transformational relationships. And so, we have decided to write this book.

As twin flames and soul mates ourselves, we know how harrowing the journey of mutual spiritual awakening can be. We know with intimate precision what ecstasies, agonies, and horrors are found on the path of spiritual partnership. Since our union on November 11, 2011, we have experienced tremendous highs, unfathomable lows, and numerous shared mystical experiences together. We know the danger that lies in spiritual partnerships, and the intense opportunities for growth, transformation, and self-fulfillment. We know what shadows limit the blossoming of spiritual partnerships, and what tools can be used to transmute and overcome such demons lurking in the dark. Most of all, we know how to help you achieve the ultimate potential of soul mate and twin flame relationships: to create *large scale* changes within yourself and the world around you through the power of love.

Back in 2011, we knew nothing of twin flame relationships. We had heard of *soul mate* relationships, but that was about it. Almost ten years later we have experienced the privilege of creating a "spiritual child" together in the form of a large website that is visited by over 10 million people a year – many of which visit our twin flame articles and have benefited from the guidance tremendously. After discovering the concept of twin flames a couple of years after our relationship ignited we decided to write a few articles about it, not thinking much of it. Years later, we have received an estimated three thousand or more emails and comments from people all throughout the world seeking help and guidance. We have heard remarkable stories of divine timing and synchronicity, as well as heartbreaking stories of breakup, loss, and death. We have also created a twin flame group on the social media platform Facebook that, at the time of writing, has tens of thousands of members. We have mentored, individually coached, and given advice to many couples who have suffered and struggled to keep their spiritual partnerships afloat. But still, there is an ever-increasing demand for help and guidance that a handful of articles or talks on the internet can never completely fulfill. Although we were reluctant to write a book on the topic at first, we can no longer put off presenting a more in-depth exploration of twin flame and soul mate relationships to the world.

This book has been designed to answer the majority of your questions and provide clear actionable solutions where necessary on the topic of soul mates and twin flames. However, we cannot claim sole credit for this book: it has been produced through the collective effort of thousands of individuals and couples who have reached out to us for support and shared their stories over the years. Without this exchange of energy and information, this book could have never materialized.

So with the knowledge that this book is a product of the Universal Mind wanting to make itself heard, may the words within these pages provide you with understanding, clarity, hope, joy, and peace. May you and your sacred relationship be blessed.

The supreme state of human love

is the unity of one soul within two bodies.

– Sri Aurobindo

CHAPTER 1

Love and the Spiritual Awakening Process

It is an absolute human certainty that no one can know his own beauty or perceive a sense of his own worth until it has been reflected back to him in the mirror of another loving, caring human being.

– JOHN JOSEPH POWELL

If you desire to find true, meaningful, and deep soul mate or twin flame love, chances are you have gone through – or are about to experience – the process of *spiritual awakening*.

"What is spiritual awakening?" you may wonder. Put simply, spiritual awakenings mark the beginning of your initiation on the spiritual path. When you undergo a spiritual awakening you literally "wake up" to life. You may begin to question your old beliefs, habits, and social conditioning, and see that there is much more to life than been taught. You may start to ask deep as "what is the purpose of my life?" "what we die?" and "why am I so unhappy?" Your mind will begin to have spiritual revelations and life-changing insights.

But the spiritual awakening process is far more complicated than thinking, questioning, or pondering about metaphysical topics. The process of waking up is multi-layered and cyclical. It is a time of death and rebirth, a time of endings and new beginnings, and a time of letting go and inviting in. When we go through a spiritual awakening our old self is stripped away, our priorities crumble, and our goals and dreams fade away. We may feel confused, scared, and depressed. But we'll also feel rejuvenated, joyful, and blissfully expanded.

Perhaps one of the hardest parts of the spiritual awakening process is the sense of loneliness and alienation we feel. We may lose touch with old friends and family members. We may desire to quit our jobs and pursue something more meaningful. We may become hermits who hide from the world because it feels too overwhelming. We might even touch the depths of the emptiness we carry inside and go through an intense life crisis.

But although the spiritual awakening process ca[n turn] our world inside out, it blesses us in so many ways. We may discover our hidden gifts, feel more connected to nature, develop a healing relationship with our soul, feel more in tune with our intuition, undergo mystical experiences of Oneness, and desire to help the world at large. At some point, we'll come to understand how profoundly important it is to connect with someone who truly sees, loves, and accepts us. And thus, the desire to find one's soul mate or twin flame is ignited.

The more we progress on our spiritual paths, the more we may realize, on a deep level, that we are destined to meet someone, but we don't know who – and we don't know *how* to get there (which can be tremendously frustrating!). Furthermore, the more spiritually connected we become, the more we may intuitively sense that *finding our soul mate or twin flame is not only important, but it is actually part of our life purpose.* We may understand that on a deep level, our soul seeks expansion, and the best way to do that is within the loving container of a relationship.

It's also possible to undergo a spiritual awakening *after* being in a soul mate or twin flame relationship. If this is the case, we may have experienced disturbing inner shifts as a result of being so close to another human being. We may have received past life flashbacks, repetitive dreams, or other alarming synchronicities. Or we may have even gone through a profoundly distressing breakup that shattered our world, but at the same time, opened the spiritual floodgates.

Regardless of whether you're single or are currently in a relationship, it is essential for you to understand how mighty and transformative soul mate and twin flame relationships can be. Wanting to find true love is not for the faint of heart! These two relationships, while serving slightly different purposes, are both united in their ability to crack you open and kindle bone-deep transformation. You will *not* be the same person after entering a soul mate or twin flame relationship – that much can be assured! But although the changes you will undergo can feel threatening to the ego, they are real nourishment to the soul.

Soul mate and twin flame relationships are perhaps one of the most powerful vehicles of spiritual awakening in existence. They challenge you on every level, demand that you grow and become all that you're destined to be – all in a loving and nurturing space. We'll explore how to use your relationship as a catalyst for true spiritual transformation later in the book. But first, let's dive into the mysterious world of soul mates and twin flames. What exactly are they? What's the difference between them? And what gifts can they offer you? Turn the page to find out.

"I've always believed that soul mates exist and they come in various forms. However, in my case, I've always felt like I was born in the wrong place and at the wrong time. I do believe that my soul mate is on the other side of the planet right now. I also believe that there's an invisible rope connecting us together and that, someday, somehow, we will meet and our souls will become whole again."

– CAMERON (shared on lonerwolf.com)

CHAPTER 2

What is a Soul Mate?

So, what is a soul mate? And is it true that we *all* have one that we are destined to meet? I bet you've thought about this question at least once before.

When most of us picture a soul mate couple, we tend to think of Romeo and Juliet, Tristan and Isolde, or Elizabeth Bennet and Mr. Darcy, and the intense, passionate, and whirlwind romance that defined their relationships. But while these exciting and often tragic love stories gave us a glimmer of hope that our own love stories could be just as enchanting, in reality, we struggle with romances that are lackluster at best, and utterly incompatible at worst.

There are so many misconceptions about soul mates out there that are caused by wishful thinking and idealism. To most people (and maybe even you too), soul mates are generally thought to be people who stick by your side forever – we're talking your *entire lifespan*. They're also idealized as people who complete you and make your life better than it once was.

What is true and what is false? In our experience, here is what truly defines a soul mate:

1. Soul mates are your best friends. They're also your romantic and sexual partners. (You can also have deep platonic connections with friends, family members, and animals).

2. Soul mates are your spiritual catalysts. They don't complete you, but they do help you to become the best version of yourself possible. Why don't they complete you? Because you are already complete at your core, and throughout your life, you are in the process of rediscovering that.

3. Soul mates are your confidants and teachers. Sometimes the lessons they teach are intentional, but often the lessons they teach are unintentional and are a byproduct of your relationship with them. Because they understand you so profoundly, soul mates also make powerful confidants, helping you through tough times and inspiring you to do and be your very best.

4. Soul mates feel very 'familiar.' This feeling of familiarity likely occurs because your souls have spent many past lives together. Something between the two of you just clicks, as though you have been friends or lovers forever.

5. Soul mates can often see parts of you that you aren't even aware of. Therefore, they're able to point out aspects of your personality for you to become mindful of (which may shock or unsettle you). While these revelations can feel uncomfortable, they're also extremely beneficial as they help you to develop authentic self-awareness.

6. Soul mates vibrate at the same frequency as you. This is just a fancy way of saying that soul mates not only share your likes, tastes, and goals, but they also share your deeper life values, beliefs, and dreams. You both "get" each other on a DNA level.

7. Soul mates love you deeply. You also love them deeply. Although it may not be possible for soul mates always to stay together, it is impossible for soul mates to harbor feelings of hatred for each other for long periods. Despite what they do, you still love them, and they still love you.

8. Soul mates aren't perfect. They have their flaws, gross habits, and strange quirks, but these qualities don't repel you as your connection goes much deeper than the average relationship. Despite your mutual imperfections, you both value each other at a core level.

9. Soul mates aren't always immediately recogn Love at first sight isn't a myth, but it also isn't the on , way you can discover who your soul mate is. Often soul mates appear in various unexpected disguises in our lives.

10. Soul mates don't always stay with you for a lifetime. This is an extremely harmful myth that I'd love to squash once and for all! Soul mates don't always stay until the end, but this is not a bad thing. We humans like to think that our lovers will be there forever because it is a comforting and sentimental thought. But sometimes life has a different plan for us. Besides, the belief that our soul mates will stay with us forever can (and often does) lead to stagnant complacency and can be a big obstacle for inner growth.

Unfortunately, the idea that soul mates "should" stay with us forever has wrought an unfathomably large amount of misery in people's lives. The key thing to remember is that sometimes soul mates are there for only a season, and sometimes they are there for a lifetime. But whatever the case, enjoy the ride.

11. There is the possibility of finding multiple soul mates. Unlike twin flames, we have many soul mates. However, it must be emphasized here that most people only tend to find one or two soul mates who they're deeply compatible with across the span of a lifetime.

The Role of Soul Mates

Soul mates are people in our lives whom we connect to on a deep level. As the name implies, soul mates are primarily friends of the soul. If you have found your soul mate they will likely be the best, and truest friend, you will ever have. You'll be able to share everything with your soul mate, from your wildest dreams to your most shameful secrets. Nothing is off limits.

Spiritually, soul mates usually play a significant role in your development. It is possible for soul mates to be platonic, romantic and/or sexual in nature. You can also have multiple soul mates in one lifetime, hence the many love triangles we see and experience.

Ultimately, a soul mate is a member of your soul family. They are the souls that come into your life for one reason or another, and they can be anyone – from a family member to a close friend, colleague, neighbor, child, or romantic partner.

We all have a soul, and when we encounter other souls in our lives, the friction of two energy forces colliding with such intimacy and vulnerability can create challenging effects. Some souls will feel as known each other for lifetimes, some will will feel at ease with the other person's company.

Soul mates serve as mirrors of ourselves. What we see in another soul reflects that which is contained within our own soul. Some of the souls that come into our lives will help us grow in love and wisdom, while others will aid us in learning painful life lessons or universal truths. We'll explore the idea of different soul connections later on in this chapter.

No matter how fleeting the encounter, each soul that comes into our lives has the potential to provide a significant life-transforming moment; even that one girl that smiled at you from the window of a bus passing by.

Do We *All* Have Soul Mates?

This is a difficult question to answer because it depends on your level of mental, emotional, and spiritual maturity.

Can a reactive, materialistic and self-hating person stuck in old patterns of dogmatic belief and fear-driven world perceptions find a soul mate? *It isn't likely.* Why? Because in order to authentically give love, you must first have some amount of self-love. And in order to welcome the unsettling changes and ego-dissolution that soul mates bring, you need to be in an open-minded, receptive and trusting place.

I believe that everyone has at least one soul friend in life, and we all have many soul teachers (we'll explore these concepts later), but soul mates are another story.

Attracting a person into your life who is genuinely compatible with you requires inner work. How can you discover who your soul mate is without first knowing who you really are and what you really want out of life? You'll always be clambering around in the dark.

This is the precise reason why so many people struggle to find "The One" in their lives: their abject lack of self-knowledge, self-understanding, and self-love prevents them. So many of us carry this belief that someone or something else outside of ourselves will "complete us" when all along the answers lie within us. Soul mates just help us to realize this by opening our hearts through the power of love.

So our answer is this: we all have the *opportunity* to find soul mates, but we don't always have the *capacity*. To illustrate this further: how can I understand what a soul mate is if I don't yet have any understanding of my soul? How can I experience the deep love of a soul mate union when I continue to hate myself and other people?

Of course, I'm not saying that we have to be perfect or enlightened to find our soul mates, but we *do* need to be actively undergoing the process of spiritual evolution.

The truth is that our mindsets and values determine our reality. If I have the mindset of being poor and destitute, my emotional life will reflect that. If I value fame, status, and money, my reality will reflect that whether it be through my big million dollar mansion or my impoverished relationships – or both. If, on the other hand, I value love, connection, and spiritual growth, my life will mirror that on all levels.

Different Types of Soul Connections

In our language, we have the word "friend," and the word "soul mate." But how would you describe someone that falls *in between*? What about someone who is more than just a best friend but doesn't have the romantic and sexual attraction as a stereotypical soul mate?

We need new words to express the complex relationships that we have with others. Here are a few words that will help you to distinguish between the different types of soul connections you may develop across the course of your lifetime:

Soul Friend

This is your most common type of soul connection. A Soul Friend is a person in your life who you've chosen because your ego/identity is harmonious with the other's character. Essentially, you share the same tastes, interests, beliefs, sense of humor, and values.

While this connection is not as deep as a Soul Companion, a Soul Friend's company creates little friction. Sometimes Soul Friends can become Soul Teachers, but generally, *you* are the one who chooses your Soul Friend as you perceive the world in a similar way to them.

Soul Teacher

Soul Teachers are composed of all the people in your life that have come to teach you a lesson. They don't necessarily teach you intentionally, but instead often provide challenging situations in your life for you to overcome and learn from.

Soul Teachers often come in the form of family members, friends, acquaintances, old lovers, momentary drifters, and even enemies. You attract them into your life because you need to learn something from them.

For example, some teach you to cultivate patience for the guy who doesn't signal before changing lanes, others teach you to stop lusting over the "bad boys" that keep crossing your path, and others help you to develop greater compassion and understanding for other beliefs and cultures.

Usually, any friction in relationships is due to a failure in acknowledging something within ourselves, or in other words, a resistance to the lessons our Soul Teachers teach us. We can never change other people unless *they* are open to changing, but we can change *ourselves*.

Soul Companion

This would come closest to what we commonly define as a "soul mate" with the exception of romantic attraction. Soul Companions can be males or females, friends or family members. While Soul *Friends* are compatible with us on mostly an ego level, Soul *Companions* experience deeper compatibility with us on a soul level. Therefore, Soul Companions tend to stick around a lot longer in our lives than Soul Friends.

Many times it feels as though we've known our Soul Companions for centuries, even from past lives. With a Soul

...re is a great and deep understanding of the... ...a feeling that you are both on the same... ...thoughts and emotions. These connections often last for a lifetime.

Soul Companions share both attributes of Soul Friends and Soul Teachers in that they experience ego harmony with us, as well as teach, guide, and support us on our journeys – except there is little friction with them unlike with Soul Teachers. Instead, Soul Companions lovingly share the life journey with us. One of the reasons why we feel such depth of harmony with them is because they usually share with us the same level of emotional, mental, and spiritual maturity.

Soul Mate

Finding our Soul Mate often feels like finding a piece of ourselves that was missing. Many describe the feeling as "returning home" or developing a greater sense of wholeness in the presence of the other person.

Soul Mates share complementary, compatible life goals and their spiritual natures are often in sync with ours. They also experience an immense level of comfort with each other that cannot be experienced in other relationships, and they

complement each other in many ways thro[ugh]
strengths and weaknesses.

So that's it. We've now broken down the four different types of soul connections.

In the end, it's important to remember that none of these relationships are better or worse than the other – they each serve a purpose in our spiritual growth and healing.

Why Soul Mates Come Into Our Lives

There are three ways a soul mate can come into our lives, and that is: *for a reason, for a season and for a lifetime.*

It is essential to understand this distinction. Once you know *why* a soul mate has come into your life, you'll know what to expect from that connection. Let's take a closer look at the reasons why soul mates come into our lives:

For a Reason

When you come across a soul mate for a reason, it's usually to meet an urgent need of yours. This need can be for guidance, assistance through difficult times, support, or simply deep companionship.

For a Season

Next, there are soul mates for a season – or people that come into your life only momentarily. These people serve as catalysts, guides, teachers, and supporters to help you grow and learn. They may present themselves in a moment when you need to overcome a core fear, challenge a limiting belief, release a deep trauma, or discover what your life passion is. Regardless of the reason or situation, these soul mates are only seasonal and leave once their gift has passed on.

For a Lifetime

Finally, there are lifetime soul mate relationships. These connections teach us lessons that are so deep and intricate that they require a lifetime of loving growth with the other to assimilate deeply.

In lifetime connections, the strengths and weaknesses of each partner balance the other's out perfectly. This delicate equilibrium within the relationship opens a space for learning and assimilating the other's qualities. The more each partner can learn from the other, the more inner balance is created, and the more spiritual transformation occurs. Usually, the harmony between both soul mates is so deep that it flows into a lifetime spent together.

Lifetime relationships are as rare and precious as fine jewels, and we should feel immensely blessed if we encounter them during our lives.

Finding Your Soul Mate

There are many soul mates out there that we have the opportunity to encounter during our lives. While some come to teach us something new, others come to share our joys. While some last for only a few months or years, others last for a lifetime.

With these lessons and shared moments of bliss, we learn to grow spiritually and come closer to finding our wholeness as human beings.

In a later chapter, we'll explore how to find your soul mate. But first, let's move on to exploring twin flames relationships and the key differences between them and soul mate connections.

"Years ago, I met someone whom I developed a great love for. I can't begin to describe the depth of those feelings. Since then, I have come to love others, but there was something innately different about those relationships. This person was like a bright burning flame, the kind of incredible, unforgettable person you only meet once in your life. Our feelings developed quickly and we instantly connected."

– ROBERT (sent via email)

CHAPTER 3

What is a Twin Flame?

The moment you meet your twin flame is the moment the earth beneath your feet begins to shift.

We like to think of the meeting of two twin flames as an existential earthquake: all of a sudden you can sense that an immensely important person has entered your life. All of a sudden you get the overwhelming feeling that your life is going to change in a way you aren't even aware of yet – and yet you intuitively know that the changes will be great, greater than what you've ever experienced and breathtaking in their magnitude.

The opportunity to connect with a twin flame is open to everyone. However, such a gift is not always openly received or even recognized by us on a conscious level. Sometimes we're at a point in our lives where we're simply not receptive to both ourselves and our twin flame's presence due to stress, over-work, lifestyle habits and negative thought patterns that lead to low self-esteem.

In this chapter, we'll explore what a twin flame is, the origin of the twin flame concept, signs you're in a twin flame relationship, the purpose of twin flame relationships, and the eight stages of twin flame connection.

What is a Twin Flame?

Firstly, let's define what a twin flame is. Hopefully, this will help to give you some clarity.

Your twin flame, or twin soul, is a person who you are destined to feel connected to on a physical, emotional, mental, and spiritual level. A twin flame is a person who is your friend, lover, and teacher in this life. He or she is the catalyst of your spiritual growth and the mirror of your deepest desires, needs, and fears. Your twin flame will reflect back to you all of your inner shadows, but also your deepest beauty and greatest strengths. In this way, your twin flame helps you to access tremendous emotional, psychological, and spiritual growth.

The main difference between twin flames and soul mates is the fact that in a twin flame relationship you will be continuously challenged to grow, shed your ego, and awaken. While soul mates are loving companions, twin flames are the fires that burn through our fears, limiting beliefs.

Twin Flame Signs

Whatever our souls are made of, his and mine are the same.

– EMILY BRONTË

As mentioned previously, we are not always receptive to the appearance of our twin flames in life. We might be heart-broken, wracked with grief, maritally over-burdened, or just plain tired and disillusioned when they suddenly appear out of the blue. In fact, we might have already *met* our twin flames, but we might have overlooked them or taken them for granted in some way.

Whatever emotional or psychological stage you're at in life, it's always beneficial to be conscious of the people you live with and meet. If you're curious about twin flames and want to know whether you've met one (or are with one), pay attention to the following signs. Keep in mind that some of these signs will emerge immediately, while others may take months or years to arise:

1. *You feel a strange, inexplicable sense of "recognition" when you meet the person.* This might manifest as déjà vu, or

an unshakable feeling that you've known this person before, or are somehow "meant to be together." (When Luna and I first got together, for example, we experienced many moments of déjà vu, sometimes coinciding at the exact same moment alongside each other.)

2. *You have a feeling that they are going to play a crucial role in your own development,* without knowing when, why or how.

3. *You've established an immediate, intense connection* with them that is invigorating and shocking at the same time.

4. *You feel as though you've finally found a "home"* or safe place with the other person.

5. *You can be your authentic self* – warts and all – without the fear of rejection, persecution or judgment around them.

6. *You both embody the yin and yang,* in other words, your dark side is balanced by their light side, and their dark side is balanced by your light side, and vice versa.

7. *You feel a sense of expansion with them,* as though you are larger than your limited identity.

8. *They make you a better person,* and you make them a better person.

9. *When together you are both bonded but free, attached but unattached.* In other words, you still maintain your freedom even though you might be in a relationship with them.

10. *You are finely tuned to their energy,* and they are finely tuned to yours. This means that you are both very conscious of the present play of energy (whether happy or sad, angry or forgiving, open or withholding) present in your connection. You're both therefore highly empathic with each other.

11. *You feel as though you have been waiting for this person your entire life.*

12. *You both connect deeply* and mirror each other's values and aspirations for life beyond surface similarities.

13. *Your twin flame is a mirror of what you fear and simultaneously desire the most for your own inner healing.* For example, if you are a highly-strung person, your twin flame will most likely be relaxed and carefree. If you like to play the victim, your twin flame will be a strong character who refuses to give you pity or sympathy to perpetuate your unhealthy habits. If you

are creatively repressed, your twin flame will be a flourishing artist. In this way, our twin flames challenge and infuriate us but also teach us valuable lessons about our fears, core wounds, and repressions.

14. *Your childhoods were polar opposite.* You were raised in very different ways, which led to the development of opposite childhood wounds that you now have the opportunity to mend.

15. *One of you is more spiritually mature than the other* and often serves as the teacher, counselor or confidant within the relationship. (Please note that this dynamic usually changes throughout the relationship.)

16. *You are taught important life lessons* such as forgiveness, gratitude, empathy, and open-mindedness by them and alongside them.

17. *Your connection is multi-faceted.* In other words, your twin flame is likely your best friend, lover, teacher, nurturer, and muse all at once.

18. *The most growth you've ever experienced has been with them.* No other friendship or relationship has transformed you as deeply as this one has.

19. *Your twin flame doesn't try to change you.* They accept you for who you are and what stage you're at and encourage you to do the same for yourself (and vice versa).

20. *You can be truthful with each other about anything.*

21. *Together, you both feel driven towards a higher purpose,* whether spiritually, socially or ecologically.

Our twin flames can be friends or lovers. For some people, they arise at the most opportune times, and for others, they arise at the most complicated times. And still, for some people twin flames are said to not arise in this lifetime but are nevertheless with us in heart.

Whatever the case, remember that it is entirely possible to be whole and complete unto yourself. It is important to stress here that twin flames do not "complete" you because you are already innately "complete" at a soulful level. Instead, they *compliment* you deeply and help you to grow.

Furthermore, the phrase "twin flame relationship" isn't meant to be another word for codependency and emotional enmeshment – as is often falsely depicted on the media and internet. It is vital to fly free within your relationship and not expect your twin flame to meet every single one of your needs. Desiring your twin flame to "be your everything" places too much pressure on the relationship, causing it to wither and potentially self-destruct.

When Luna and I first got together I gave her a ring with the inscription "Alis Volat Propriis" or *she flies with her own wings*. I gave her this to symbolize my desire to enter a conscious relationship; one where instead of being her captor I would be the beholder of her growth and transformation.

It's a sad reality, but in our relationships as a species, we treat each other as objects to be owned and possessed. But once we do manage to cage or "secure" our partners to "be our everything," we suffer horribly. Once we metaphorically capture that beautiful bird we were initially attracted to, we feel guilty every time the bird chirps: we are reminded that we've taken away the very thing that made the bird so beautiful in the first place.

As Austrian poet and novelist Rainer Maria Rilke writes, "The point of marriage is not to create a quick commonality by tearing down all boundaries; on the contrary, a good marriage is one in which each partner appoints the other to be the guardian of his solitude, and thus they show each other the greatest possible trust. A merging of two people is an impossibility, and where it seems to exist, it is a hemming-in, a mutual consent that robs one party or both parties of their fullest freedom and development. But once the realization is accepted that even between the closest people infinite distances exist, a marvelous living side-by-side can grow up for them, if they succeed in loving the expanse between them, which gives them the possibility of always seeing each other as a whole …"

As we can see, freedom is a core value within twin flame relationships (and indeed *all* types of relationships). Without freedom, there can be no spiritual transformation, which is the goal of all twin flame connections. We'll explore more of these relationship shadows in chapters nine and ten.

11 Signs You're in a Twin Flame Relationship

The opportunity to find true love is open to all people. And one of the most sacred vehicles of this journey towards experiencing true love is the twin flame union.

If you're currently in a relationship and would like to know whether you're in a twin flame relationship, read the signs below.

Remember, a twin flame relationship is not better or more superior than other relationships. All types of relationships, twin flame or not, have their own spiritual

The twin flame connection may appear more than other types of relationships due to its intensity, but it's not for the faint of heart.

With that being said, here are eleven signs you're in a twin flame relationship:

1. There's the sensation that time doesn't exist between you.

2. You both feel a strange sense of "recognition" or déjà vu between you as though you're both "destined" to be together.

3. You have an intense magnetic attraction to each other.

4. You both trigger each other's shadows, wounds, and fears to a large and sometimes overwhelming degree.

5. Your strengths and weaknesses perfectly balance each other.

6. You share the same values, desires, and dreams.

7. Your flame knows you better than anyone else in the world.

8. You have a multi-faceted connection together, i.e., you are best friends, teachers, and lovers to each other.

9. Uncanny synchronicities exist between you (e.g., you keep experiencing repetitive numbers, unlikely omens, and bizarre synchronicities).

10. You're both driven towards a higher spiritual or social purpose.

11. Together, you both learn the values of empathy, compassion, forgiveness, and unconditional love.

The more signs you can relate to, the more likely you are in a twin flame relationship.

The Origins of Twin Flames

And so, when a person meets the half that is his very own, whatever his orientation, whether it's to young men or not, then something wonderful happens: the two are struck from their senses by love, by a sense of belonging to one another, and by desire, and they don't want to be separated from one another, not even for a moment. – PLATO

The concept of having a "Twin Flame" originated in Plato's mythic dialogue entitled *The Symposium* which wrote that n beings originally had two faces, four arms, and four Under the threat of being overpowered, the gods split them in half, creating the humans we see today. Hence, it is thought that we all have one "twin" soul out there in the world.

Others hypothesize that twin flames are members of our Soul Group (people whom we resonate with on the deepest level and are predestined to meet), or that twin flames are the embodiment or other "half" of a singular soul.

However, *we define twin flames as those whose souls have agreed to reincarnate together across many lifetimes for the sake of personal and global enlightenment.* Like two tuning forks or gravitational fields, twin flames are magnetically attracted to each other. This magnetic attraction might be because everything is composed of energy at its core, and twin flames are the people we most closely resonate with.

The Purpose of Twin Flame Relationships

Put simply, the purpose of the twin flame union is to help each other spiritually grow, expand, and reach spiritual illumination. In other words, twin flame relationships exist to help us shed away the snakeskin of the ego, face and heal our wounded hearts, and transform into awakened beings.

Twin flame partnerships are meant to develop into divine beacons of Balance, Harmony, and Love. Ultimately, most twin flame couples will have a higher purpose to achieve together, and this may include anything from raising conscious children to stepping into a role that helps to revolutionize society.

Contrary to popular belief, twin flames do not complete each other– this is because the soul itself is already complete. Instead, such relationships exist to catalyze spiritual maturing and conscious expansion. In other words, twin flame connections exist to aid the collective growth of our planet towards compassion, tranquility, and love.

On a personal level, twin flame relationships prepare us to acknowledge, experience and eventually embody the Wholeness that has always and forever been inside of us. This state of Wholeness is what enlightened teachers through the ages have integrated and spoken about. This Wholeness is the soul or True Self within us.

Ascended Twin Flames

What about those of us who sense that our twin flames are currently not residing on this planet? This is where the notion of the ascended twin flame comes in.

Ascended twin flames are our spiritual counterparts who have done the inner work and undergone enlightenment (or "ascension") in a previous lifetime. It is helpful to remember that many twin flames are ascended and are waiting for their divine counterparts to join them. The best thing we can do in this lifetime to unite with our twin flame is to do the work and walk the spiritual path. If your twin flame has ascended, you are never alone. Although your twin flame may not be with you in body, they are there with you in spirit.

Is it still possible to connect with an ascended twin flame? Yes, it is. The best way is to use methods that temporarily weaken the ego and allow the higher forces to come through. Examples include meditation, visualization, pathworking, scrying, dream work, and other methods that induce altered states of consciousness. You can use these methods to seek guidance and support from your twin flame or simply to be in their presence.

Perhaps the most pressing question is this: how do you know that you have an ascended twin flame versus an earthly twin flame? The best way to know is to sit quietly somewhere undisturbed and focus on the area of your heart. Relax your body and take some mindful breaths. When you feel a sense of stillness inside, quietly ask your heart "is my twin flame living on earth or have they ascended?" Wait for a response.

If you feel a tugging, pulling or heavy sensation in your heart area, your twin flame is most likely still living on this planet. If you feel a sense of calmness, spaciousness, and lightness, your twin flame has most likely ascended. Your heart and body carry deep wisdom: they are mirrors of what you know and possess deep down, so don't be afraid to tune into them.

If you need extra clarification, try the dream incubation method. Half an hour before you go to sleep, think about your twin flame. You might wish to draw a picture, listen to a twin flame meditation, or anything that primes your unconscious mind with the topic of twin flames. You may like to repeat a mantra such as "*on earth or ascended?*" over and over again. Go to sleep with a sense of expectancy. If you believe that you'll have a revelatory dream, you most likely will as the mind is highly influenced by belief. When you wake up, record any significant dreams you've had. Did you dream of meeting a person in your workplace, in nature, or somewhere on earth? If so, your twin flame is likely here in-the-flesh. If, on the other hand, you dreamt of meeting an angelic being, floating up into the clouds, or otherwise finding yourself in a strange otherworldly location, your twin flame is likely ascended. Your dreams don't just help your brain to make sense of waking life, they also unite us with deeper truths and realities.

Stages of Twin Flame Love

Twin flames, whether earthly or ascended, help to aid our souls in finding completion. However, this journey is often composed of many different "layers" or stages we must move through within this lifetime.

Here are the eight major twin flame stages which are broken down and summarized below:

1. **Yearning For "The One"** – This stage is spent preparing for your twin flame on an emotional and psychological level. Often, a certain level of individuation and healthy self-esteem must be developed before meeting your flame.

2. **Glimpsing "The One"** – In this stage, you'll temporarily glimpse or come in contact with your twin flame. This experience might be through a dream, a picture, or through brief real-life contact.

3. **Falling in Love** – After finally meeting your twin flame, you will fall rapidly, deeply, and madly in love. You might try to resist the experience at first perhaps due to an already established relationship, but eventually, you won't be able to stay away from them.

4. The Fairy-Tale Relationship – After deciding to enter a relationship, you'll enter a dream-like period that feels like paradise. Everything will feel perfect within your relationship.

5. Outer Turmoil and Inner Purging – As the sparkle from your new love wears off, egos begin to rise up. In this stage, any insecurities, fears, traumas, and shadow issues buried within you and your partner will come to the surface. These will need to be resolved for you to mature as a couple.

6. The Runner and Chaser – Like stage five, this stage is a "trial by fire." As tensions mount, it is common to temporarily (or in some extreme cases, permanently) leave the relationship either emotionally or physically. The less mature and psychospiritually integrated partner will play the role of the Runner, while the more emotionally balanced partner will play the Chaser. This game of cat and mouse can last for days to years.

7. Surrender and Dissolution – Eventually, issues are resolved in your relationship, and a space of acceptance and openness is established. (Please note that this stage is not always reached by all twin flame couples.)

8. Oneness – The more shadows are dealt with, the easier Unity becomes. In this stage, twin flames experience conflict and a return to blissful paradise. Often, focus extends beyond the boundaries of their relationship to the external world and how they can help and serve humanity.

It's important to note here that these twin flame stages are not always linear. Sometimes they overlap, and occasionally certain stages are skipped and revisited. In the runner and chaser stage, it's also possible to change roles. Ultimately, it's crucial to understand that the twin flame relationship is like any living and breathing entity: it goes through cycles of evolution. It's okay to change and grow, in fact, it's essential!

The False Twin Flame

The concept of having a "false twin flame" has been increasing in popularity over the past few years. Is it true that we can have false twin flames? Absolutely.

The complicated and often times dangerous reality of falling in love is that our heart can override our reason. We may be so blinded by our infatuations or projections that we fail to see the truth and fail to tune into the red flags. Those who discover that they have false twin flames often awaken to reality after their hearts are crushed, their trust is broken, or they are otherwise subjected to extreme forms of abuse that would clearly not come from a real twin flame.

Signs of the false twin flame relationship include the following:

- They are not interested in spiritual growth
- They shame or criticize you for wanting to grow
- They hide who they truly are and wear "two faces"
- They play psychological games with you
- They don't share your deepest values
- They don't share a common vision with you
- They encourage self-destruction and bad habits
- They make you feel like your authentic self is not good enough
- They repeatedly betray your trust or lie to you without remorse

While a false twin flames relationship can cause you to feel small, alone, empty, and even crazy (if the person was a narcissist), there is a hidden gift. False twin flame relationships help us to understand ourselves better. They are a powerful lesson in the importance of being discerning, self-caring, and aware of our shadows. The reason why we enter false twin flame relationships in the first place is due to the naivety of romanticizing others and being disconnected from the wisdom of our soul.

How can we prevent ourselves from falling into false twin flame relationships? The easiest answer is to go slowly. Allow yourself a little room to feel caution. It's okay to be protective of your own heart. Take time to observe the person, ask them questions, test their responses, and most importantly, their sincerity. Do they share the same values as you? Do they seem authentic? Or does something feel a bit "off"? Can you find any strange examples of behavior that seem to be inconsistent? Don't close your eyes to these discrepancies just because your feelings of dizzy lovesick excitement seem so delicious and strong.

Examples of incongruous "red flag" behavior include saying one thing and doing another, taking delight in harming others, always drawing the conversation back to themselves, disinterest in personal growth, extreme sensitivity to criticism, delusions of grandeur, and a sense of entitlement. This list is by no means exhaustive, so don't take it as gospel. Remember to use your heart, mind, *and* soul when getting to know a prospective twin flame.

Spiritual Alchemy

Twin flames are the living embodiments of spiritual alchemy. When we get into a relationship with our flame, we are getting into a relationship with a force of nature. In alchemy, this is known as *coniunctio* or the marriage of opposites.

Perhaps what is most unique about the twin flame relationship is the element of transformation or alchemy that occurs within us. Don't expect to stay the same person when you find your twin flame! So much will shift, dissolve, and expand within you that it can get overwhelming sometimes. Perhaps the most important quality to bring to the twin flame union is receptivity and the willingness to surrender all limiting beliefs, wounds, and fears that are holding us back. That is no easy task! But it is possible, particularly when you're evolving alongside another person.

By now you should have a good understanding of the twin flame relationship. We have explored a lot in this chapter, including the interesting topics of ascended and false twin flames. You're welcome to refer back to this chapter if you need help identifying what stage you're at in your partnership or how to recognize your twin flame in the first place.

In the next chapter we'll share a little about our own twin flame story, including how we met, the initial difficulties we faced, and how we overcame them.

Let us be like

Two falling stars in the day sky.

Let no one know of our sublime beauty

As we hold hands with God

And burn into a sacred existence that defies

— That surpasses —

Every description of ecstasy

And love.

— Hafiz

CHAPTER 4

The Story of Luna and Sol

The story began in 2011. We were both in our early twenties and were shy, inexperienced in love, and entirely unprepared for the soul-igniting relationship that is twin flame love. From the beginning, our lives and upbringings were completely opposite — almost to a comical extent. We weren't just "chalk and cheese," we were from completely different universes it seemed.

Having constantly traveled throughout his youth, Sol never developed strong roots to any single place until he moved to Australia in 2004. His childhood was full of the excitement of drifting between Spain and India, but the profound chaos, horror, and heartbreak of living with an uncle who struggled with schizophrenia and a mother who grappled with chronic drug addiction and bipolar disorder. Sol's dad was totally absent and presumed dead throughout his childhood, so he was raised by his eclectic hippy grandparents who blessed him with the ability to t[...] live freely, even despite the pain, suffering, and insanity around him.

On the opposite end of the spectrum was my life. I grew up in Western Australia, never knowing any other place from my small, isolated city. Being raised in a fundamentalist Christian church known as the Church of Christ (CoC), I was deeply programmed and brainwashed since birth. I attended church twice a week for my entire life, sitting through thousands of hours of sermons designed to coerce and condition the mind with fear and hatred. The CoC was a non-denominational cult that believed it was the "One True Church" and thrived on isolation, scare-tactics, and righteous legalism. Extracting myself from that environment was hard. But ironically, in the end, it was my upbringing that gave me the thirst to relentlessly search for freedom, love, and truth.

Considering our completely opposite backgrounds, it was a miracle that Sol and I ever found each other.

The First Contact …

Going through a Dark Night of the Soul was the first stage of my spiritual awakening. Such an experience was almost unbearable at times. For days at a time, I would sit alone in my bedroom, often staring out the window blankly, not knowing why I felt as though I was falling into an endless abyss. At that time, I had no friends or contacts outside of the church. I had no one to talk to and no one to share my pain with — not a single soul. My parents, seemingly oblivious to what I was going through, condemned any form of questioning, exploration or freethinking, so they were emotionally severed from me. *I had no one.* The suffocating loneliness and despair I felt seemed like it would never end.

I remember, at one point, staring at the sky and praying to God with tears streaming down my face, asking him to reveal my beloved to me. I remember crying so intensely that the capillaries around my eyes burst leaving my face bruised for days. The cognitive dissonance, fear, emptiness, self-hatred, and loneliness I felt inside tormented me. This went on for many months.

One day, I made myself do something — anything — because I was sick of the pain and isolation. So I created an online group for people in Western Australia who wanted to meet up in real life. I had no idea whether anyone would join or be interested. But slowly, people trickled in. In a few weeks, about twenty people had joined, at which point I posted a blog about meeting up in person. A people agreed, and one of them was Sol.

When I first saw a picture of Sol, the world came crashing down around me. I literally froze. I didn't know what to make of him. I didn't know whether he was Native American or Spanish, but I was captivated by his eyes and energy. A strange sense of recognition was constantly flowing through me as I looked at his picture, and intuitively I knew I had made a life-changing discovery. I didn't know what was happening exactly, but I wanted to find out more about him. Everything in my life had suddenly changed in a single moment.

Thankfully, at that time Sol had a psychology blog called "Sapientology" (which he has since sold). Reading his blog, I was mesmerized. For the first time in my life, I tasted truth — a truth so clear, so illuminating, so alive, that I was enchanted. I'm quite sure the first thing I fell in love with was not only Sol's mind but his soul. His words were like the light that illuminated my darkness. For the next few hours, I read his blog posts in a rabid frenzy.

The Meeting ...

As the days drew near to the meetup, I was feeling more and more nervous. Sol and I were exchanging messages at that point, speaking for hours on end. Neither of us knew what was happening — we had never even met in person, but we felt as if we had known each other for years, even lifetimes.

The first meeting with Sol was like a blur. Although other people turned up, they were all in the periphery. Hearing Sol talk for the first time with a slight Spanish accent made my blood tingle. We were nervous, but the chemistry between us was evident. Walking side by side, we couldn't help but continuously bump into each other, as if a magnet was always drawing us together. Yet we didn't say anything of much significance that first meeting. We were too nervous and uncertain around each other.

For the next six months or so we met up with the group, spending hours talking to each other at night. We would discuss every topic under the sun. Each Sunday afternoon at 8 pm, we would turn on Skype, and talk for hours – usually six or more hours straight. The next day, I had to go to work and wake up at 5 am to leave, but after speaking with Sol, I couldn't sleep. Even though I lost sleep and suffered through tremendous anxiety at work, I didn't care. Speaking with Sol was what I looked forward to every day and what I counted down to each week. I remember how my heart would quickly beat as I ruminated on the hours of conversation we would have that went by so fast. It was as if time stood still between the two of us.

The Inner Conflict ...

One day, Sol told me that he had to travel for two weeks to attend a family wedding. Those two weeks we could barely speak at all, and they were tough, almost torturous for both of us, even though we were still friends.

During those two weeks, I had a lot of time to think. It didn't take me long to realize that I had fallen in love with Sol and that I had fallen in love with him the moment I discovered his existence.

Coming back from his trip, Sol told me that he was going to start exploring the dating world. This sent me spiraling into questions and fears. Was he hinting that he felt the same way about me? Did he only see me as a friend, and nothing more? Deep down, I was panicking. There was no way I could lose him — our connection was something powerful, intense and life-changing.

So I resolved to tell him how I felt. I remember sitting down with a pencil and notepad, shaking a little, trying to plan what to say. At the same time, I felt invigorated, as if I was finally doing something of worth. Although I was terrified of being rejected, of him not looking at me "the same way," I gathered up my courage and went ahead with my plan anyway.

I ended up telling Sol how I felt on a wintry Sunday. The moment he heard what I said, he froze, got up, and began pacing down the hallway back and forth. The world stood still for a few minutes. The silence was deafening. I could tell that I had really shocked him. After a little while, he came back, visibly bewildered but glowing. At that time, he wasn't sure how he felt, but something had changed between us. A wall had been broken, a door had opened. We decided to meet up again in a few days.

The Opening …

Until the moment I told Sol how I felt, we had always met up with other people. After my feelings were revealed, we decided to meet alone — something we had never done before. To explore how our souls interacted with each other, we decided to take a "vow of silence" so that we could experience time together without the barrier of words.

While a little quixotic, our very first moments spent together in-person involved writing silent messages to each other in a notepad. On that first unofficial date, we sat together under a tree for the first time, quietly. The energy between us mounted quickly. At that point, we had only hugged once or twice. Deep down, I knew that Sol had been wounded severely from his childhood, and wasn't accustomed to sudden expressions of heartfelt affection. But the urge burned within me like a wildfire, and leaning over suddenly, I kissed him on the cheek. He froze, and there was complete silence. Then, without warning, he gently grabbed my face and kissed me on both cheeks and forehead.

I remember explosions of emotion and a rush of energy flooding through me. We sat there for a while quietly, lost in our inner worlds, contemplating what had happened. The world of love had just opened before us. Nothing would ever be the same again.

Twin Flames 11:11

After that experience, I asked Sol on Skype if we were "still single." The thought of uniting was scary. Neither of us had ever had a serious relationship before.

We decided to make our union official on the 11.11.11 (11th of November, 2011). Back then, we had heard nothing of twin flames or the significance of 11:11 – but we liked the numbers and were delighted by the timing. Since then, we have learned the profound meaning behind this number (11:11). How strange that of all days and moments, that very day was the one carved out in our destiny!

A few days later we came together for our first date. The first day of our life together was intense, euphoric, and dream-like. As we sat under a willow tree overlooking a lake, we decided that Spirit had guided us to adopt the names "Luna" (meaning moon) and "Sol" (meaning sun). Like night and day, we had come from completely different backgrounds, yet managed to harmonize perfectly together.

Shifting slightly, Sol uttered in a low voice, "I love you, Luna." Although it was the first date, this intense declaration didn't matter to me. I knew there was something different about our connection. Feeling those words ricochet through me, I sensed that our love was the beginning of something epic.

The Disintegration …

As our worlds began to merge into one, I knew that it was time to leave my family's abusive religion forever. I remember our relationship coming close to the brink of destruction as I grappled with the thought of "going to hell forever" for loving a "sinner." Eventually, I decided that I would rather burn in hell for eternity than let a love like ours perish. The moment I decided to make that perilous leap into the literal fires of hell (in my mind) was one of the most terrifying but liberating experiences of my life.

As the months and years passed by, the extent of my deep psychological and emotional brainwashing became apparent. I was riddled with anxiety, obsessive compulsions, suicidal ideation, insecurity, dogmas, beliefs, fears, and other forms of mental illness. As Sol helped me to pry open the "Pandora's Box" of my suffering, we would often argue and fight. Our fighting became so intense that a week wouldn't pass without a severe feud, making it almost impossible for us to live with each other.

Emotionally, I was a runner, and Sol was the chaser. The feeling of having all of my beliefs and paradigms disintegrate was extraordinarily distressing and traumatizing. Instinctively, I reacted with anger, fear, and self-isolation, feeling my ego cringe in terror. But in my soul, I knew that it was all necessary for my conscious expansion.

Thankfully, my period of "deprogramming" eventually began to lessen after about three years, and for the first time, I began to see life clearly.

The Rebirth ...

After a while, it became clear that I had not only experienced a psychological rebirth but a spiritual one as well. With this new insight, I began to open myself to Sol and his loving guidance, no longer reacting from a place of fear and rage. As a result, our relationship strengthened rapidly.

Since our ecstatic and intense union, we have blessed each other immeasurably. In Sol's perspective, I gave him the opportunity to love, and be loved again truly. In my perspective, he gave me the opportunity to experience true freedom.

Since our union, we have also experienced many moments of mystical Oneness together. While we are twin flames, we also realize that it is not necessary to find love to experience Wholeness. Ironically it was our very union that helped us to discover that Wholeness is innate to who we all are – it is the natural state of each and every soul, and it is always within us, despite who we meet in life. The twin flame relationship is merely a catalyst that helps to unveil this divine revelation.

We want to thank you for being there to support the unfolding of our work through this book. We sincerely hope you benefit from the rest of these chapters as they're sourced from our direct personal discoveries and experiences with others.

In the next chapter, we'll explore how to find your own soul mate or twin flame and the three major blockages to finding love. Even if you're currently with your soul mate or twin flame, you can use the knowledge in the next chapter to strengthen your relationship and prevent it from being sabotaged by inner demons.

"For my entire life, I always thought there was a higher purpose, that something was missing from my life. My perception of love seemed complete until I met someone special who lit a fire in my heart and soul beyond the description of words. I found love, true love, the perfect storm."

— PETER (shared on lonerwolf.com)

CHAPTER 5

How to Find Your Soul Mate and Twin Flame

It's a profound question that's within the hearts and souls of most people: "How can I find true love?" Be assured that you're not alone in this longing. Also, there's a very good reason *why* your inner self desires to find love – it is a biological, emotional, psychological, and spiritual need! At a core level, you wish to be seen, understood, accepted, and loved truly for who you are. You want a companion, a best friend, a lover, a partner who will stand by you, hold your hand, and help you to become all you're destined to be. Your soul craves for love, love that leads to inner expansion and spiritual illumination.

However, in truth, we put a lot of pressure on ourselves when it comes to the quest of finding love. This pressure can compound and create blockages throughout time. We invest *so much* of our time and energy into pursuing love that we neglect our inner work. We forget that to find love, we must make ourselves someone worthy to be in a relationship with. We forget that to find love, we must first have a loving relationship with *ourselves.*

It isn't fair to our future partners (let alone anyone in our lives) to be full of bad habits, toxic mindsets, and self-destructive behaviors. That is why I say that we must make ourselves someone *worthy* to be in a relationship with. Yes, we are innately worthy at a core level. Yes, we are worthy of being loved regardless of what we say or do. But there's a difference between being innately (and objectively) lovable, and subjectively lovable in the context of a relationship. It is tiring and difficult to be around a person who has a perpetually negative attitude, low self-esteem, codependent tendencies, manipulative behaviors, and so on. It's very hard to find a healthy and mature person who would enjoy or thrive in a relationship like that!

In order to learn how to find your soul mate or twin flame, you need to first examine some of the biggest blockages to finding love. We'll examine them below.

1. You dislike yourself

The first block to finding love is low self-worth. How can we attract our soul mate or twin flame if we send out the signal to others that we "aren't good enough"? Instead of drawing in the right person, we will repel them. We won't even be able to clearly see who is good for us and who isn't. As a result, we may attract people into our lives who reinforce the negative beliefs we have about ourselves (i.e., narcissists). Low self-esteem, therefore, is the basis for toxic relationships. If we don't respect ourselves, we will have no problem with allowing others into our lives who disrespect us as well.

Low self-esteem manifests in many forms. But overall, anything that causes harm to ourselves is a sign of low self-esteem. Examples include lack of self-care, refusing to listen to our emotional needs, neglect of the body, addictions, self-harm, critical self-talk, poor confidence, and so forth. We'll explore how to remedy this issue a little later.

2. You're not being authentic

Authenticity is a word that has been used so incessantly it has almost become a cliché. But authenticity really only means *being real.* So the question must be asked, how real are you being? Are you being true to yourself in daily life? Do you even know *who* you are on a raw level?

Being inauthentic means playing a role, wearing masks, and letting others dictate your life. When you're inauthentic, you will struggle to understand yourself and your identity will be weak or fluid. You may struggle to own who you are around others, meaning that it's easy for those in your life to pressure you into being someone you're not.

Often, finding and attracting love requires tremendous vulnerability. Are you willing to be open, transparent, and real about who you are? Are you willing to be honest about your light *and* darkness? Are you willing to let someone love *all* of you – even the parts that you find ugly or shameful? If the answer is yes, authenticity isn't an issue for you. But if you hesitate to answer these questions, authenticity needs to be an area of focus for you. The best place to start is with self-love (we'll explore this more soon).

3. Your unconscious mind is undermining you

You've probably heard before that about 95% of our brain activity is unconscious, with the remaining 5% being conscious (i.e., within our awareness). This means that a whole lot is going on underneath the surface that you're not even aware of. When it comes to finding love, this can be a very detrimental thing indeed. "Why?" you may wonder. The answer is that when you're not mindful of your unconscious wounds and patterns, life feels mysterious and chaotic. For instance, you may desperately wonder why you keep getting into relationships with abusive partners. You may feel sad, frustrated, and hopeless in your ability to enact real change. But in reality, you have all the power you need – you just don't understand on a deeper level *why* you're attracting these unhealthy people.

If you find yourself falling into the same old patterns over and over again, your unconscious mind may be undermining you. Even if you don't have a history of repeating the same mistakes, your unconscious mind may still be programmed in a way that makes it extremely difficult for you to find love. For example, you might carry a deep unconscious belief from childhood that men are unsafe, and to reaffirm this belief (that's meant to protect you), you'll attract unsafe men. Or you may carry the destructive core belief that "I am a bad person" and as a result, your unconscious mind will cause you to act out and harm others unnecessarily. There are endless beliefs and scenarios out there, but the point is that your unconscious mind wields a tremendous amount of power over your waking life. It is therefore in your best interest to explore it and uproot the blockages that are preventing you from finding love. We'll explore how to do that next.

How to Attract Your Soul Mate or Twin Flame

We've just explored the three most significant blocks to finding true love. What they all have in common is the need to focus on self-development. No matter whether you're wanting to attract your twin flame or soul mate, you need to do some inner work first!

Some like to use the law of attraction to beckon true love. And while I think that's an excellent method (i.e., changing your thoughts to change your reality), for many people it doesn't go deep enough. Why? Most law of attraction techniques deal with the conscious mind; of consciously visualizing, creating vision boards, saying affirmations, and so forth. But they don't touch the depths of the unconscious mind: the realm of hidden wounds, traumas, and shadows. Understandably, it's not very appealing to "go deep" for many people as it can feel unfriendly and unfamiliar. But let me assure you that this work is absolutely worth doing. The hard path is often the best path, and while that can be difficult for some people to accept, the "proof is in the pudding." In other words, try it out for yourself and see!

Below you'll find a mixture of simple and grounded tips, as well as more complex and metaphysical forms of advice. When it comes to the inner work parts, I recommend starting with self-love first, then moving on to inner child work, and finally, shadow work. The more simple and grounded tips (practices 1-3) can be practiced as often as you like.

Practice 1: Be proactive and open

Don't shut yourself off from the world. Don't hide away. In order to find your soul mate or twin flame, you'll need to move out of your comfort zone. You don't need to jump into the deep end straight away (as that may be too overwhelming), but you do need to experiment at your own pace. This might mean going to new places, trying out new hobbies, accepting invites from friends or family members, traveling, even taking a different route to work! Start small and try one new thing each day, even if that means changing the type of jam you use on your toast in the morning. If you're a stickler for routines and find security in your habits, take pride in the little changes you make each day. You can slowly build up to big changes – but they won't feel big to you because, by that stage, you'll be used to trying new things and putting yourself out there!

Please remember that finding your soul mate or twin flame needs to be grounded in *action*. It's all fine and dandy to create elaborate visualizations, call on your spirit guides, and other practices, but the meat and bones of finding your true partner is in what you *do*. So please don't skip this step! It's essential to do *something* different, no matter how small, each day if you can.

Practice 2: Create a sacred ritual

Rituals are symbolic acts that are carried out for a particular purpose. Because rituals are symbolic, they are the perfect way to communicate with your unconscious mind and Soul. Also, the repetitive nature of rituals has a way of reinforcing your desires at a core level. And as the old truism goes, you attract what you are (or in this case, *put out*).

Like prayer, there is a lot of prejudice surrounding rituals. We tend to perceive them as being overly complex, flowery, formal, or unnecessary. If we were raised in a religious family, we might remember rituals as being boring, long-winded, pompous or confusing.

But rituals don't have to be that way. Rituals are like living art forms that *you* create and give meaning to. Remember that the function of a ritual is to symbolically communicate what *you* desire to your unconscious mind, Soul, and Spirit. Language is only one small way of conveying information. Using objects, archetypes, and images are all far more ancient ways of expressing how you feel.

To create your own love ritual, you will need to consider the following:

1. *What is the purpose of the ritual?* (What would you like to achieve and why?)
2. *How long do you plan to carry out the ritual?* (One day, one month, one year?)
3. *How much time would you like to dedicate?* (A few minutes? Half an hour? An hour?)
4. *Where and when will the ritual be held?* (In your bedroom, outside in nature, at your altar? At 6am, 12pm, 9pm?)
5. *What objects will be used in the ritual?* (A photo, a statue, a candle, etc.?)

When considering the purpose of your ritual, consider writing it down on a piece of paper. It's essential to understand *why* you're doing your ritual. If you don't know why, your ritual won't be infused with purpose, and purpose is the power, fuel, and energy that gets things moving in your deep mind and the cosmos in general.

For point two, it's helpful to set out a specific period for your ritual. While this is not mandatory, some people find that it helps to set a limit for how long they plan to carry out their rituals (particularly if they have a busy life). Others prefer to do their rituals until they intuitively sense that they're no longer needed.

Next is thinking about how long you would like your ritual to be. Again, this is not mandatory, and some people prefer to be spontaneous. But other people like to be specific and set aside, say, five minutes a day. Some even believe that the longer a ritual is, the more effective it will be due to the amount of energy you're putting in. But I don't believe this is always the case for everyone. Personally, I believe that so long as your ritual is infused with *emotion and intention,* it's dynamic.

Choosing where and when your ritual is held is important. Try to avoid busy places or environments where you don't have much privacy. A quiet corner of the room, backyard, or even in a cupboard would do. In terms of when (i.e., the time) you choose to do your ritual, try picking a moment in the day where you feel relaxed. A busy mind takes away from the power of ritual to enact real change. Consider whether you feel more relaxed in the morning, afternoon or evening.

Finally comes the fun part: selecting what you'll use in your ritual! While there is no set method, I like to structure my rituals in the following way:

- Who is involved (physically, mentally, emotionally, spiritually)?
- What is my problem or issue right now?
- What would I like changed, solved, or achieved?
- What qualities do I need? (e.g., Courage, Openness, Wisdom, etc.)
- How can I signify that the ritual is starting and finishing?

Obviously, you're welcome to do your rituals on a totally intuitive basis. But if you're a bit confused, I hope the above questions can help you out.

If you need further guidance, I'll give you an example of a ritual constructed by a fictional person seeking to find their twin flame:

Alexandra decides to do a twin flame ritual in the morning as part of her spiritual practice. She has a small altar where she keeps objects that are special to her, and it is here that she decides to do her ritual for five minutes each day.

Before doing her ritual, she must find several symbolic objects in her house. To represent herself and her future twin flame, she finds a picture of herself and a small figurine of a man. To represent her problem, which is a lack of self-love, she finds a cracked heart-shaped pebble in her backyard. To represent the qualities she needs (self-compassion, forgiveness, and trust), she uses three different crystals. And finally, to signify the opening and closing of the ritual, she rings a small bell.

In the example I've just given, our fictional person has selected a number of random objects that symbolize the essential elements of her ritual. Keep in mind that if you can't find an object to represent any element of your ritual, you can always draw it on a piece of paper or use modeling clay (like plasticine) to create an object of your own.

Like many, you might like to energetically cleanse your ritual space before you begin to create an "empty canvas." This helps to prime the mind and prepare it for something meaningful to happen (i.e., the twin flame/soul mate ritual). There are many ways to cleanse your ritual space. Some including clapping your hands, using a smudge stick, burning incense, using a singing bowl, and visualizing white light.

But what about actually *creating* the ritual? This is where you can let your intuition run wild. You might like to put the objects together in a particular order of significance, create a pattern, form a mandala, or organize them in any way that feels meaningful. If you're stuck, I recommend creating a story with your objects. For instance, on the left, you can start with the issues that are happening to you right now. Then, you can move on to the middle, which is where you would put objects that symbolize a solution. And finally, on the right, you can place the objects that signify your desired future or destination.

Play around and see what works for you. It's okay to experiment and discard what doesn't feel potent to you. Ultimately, that's the key: potency or power. When your ritual inspires, invigorates, or otherwise fills you with strong energy, you can be sure that it's working.

Practice 3: Harness the power of prayer

To some, this suggestion may be accompanied by an almighty eye-roll. But prayer doesn't have to be religious. Prayer doesn't have to be cliché. You can pray to something, or you can pray to nothing. The whole point of prayer is to openly communicate (and admit) your deepest needs and desires. Psychologically speaking, prayer – and the intensity of emotion that goes along with it – sends a strong signal to the unconscious mind. And if you practice visualization during your prayer, even better! You will be talking the language of the unconscious mind (which is symbolic/image-based) and expressing the depth of your longing through emotion. Spiritually speaking, you are letting the forces of Life know your wishes loudly and clearly!

The beauty of prayer is that it can be done at any moment. You can pray before bed, you can pray in the train station, you can pray at your desk during work, you can pray in a sacred space. Prayers can also be long or short, straightforward or poetic. Ultimately, whatever way *you* enjoy praying is the right way for you. Don't feel the need to be formal if that doesn't feel natural to you. But if being formal seems to empower your prayer, go with it!

Having a religious upbringing, I was familiar with prayer. I remember very vividly praying to meet my true love as an eighteen-year-old who was going through a severe life crisis. My praying was so intense that I went into a near-mystical trance. I was on my knees staring intensely at the light streaming through the window imploring God, the Divine, or whoever to help me. On some level, I knew that finding my twin flame was part of my larger life purpose, but at that time I wasn't sure quite what that larger purpose was. Until this day, I believe it was the intensity of that prayer that helped unite Sol and I – or at least sped up the process significantly.

So if you can muster up strong feelings, do it. If you can't, that's okay, no need to worry. Prayer can work with or without strong emotionally-fuelled petitions. Also, if you're uncomfortable with spontaneous prayer, you can always write out your prayer beforehand. Here is an example:

"Dear God/Goddess/Divine/Spirit, if it is according to the will of Life, please unite me with my soul mate/twin flame. Please help me to think and feel with clarity. May I be able to love myself so that I can truly love the one I am destined for. May I be open and receptive. Thank you for the gifts you have offered me in this life. So may it be."

You're welcome to use this prayer or alter it to your own liking if it helps.

Practice 4: Self-love

Self-love is one of the more gentle and approachable inner work paths. But that doesn't dilute or negate its importance. Self-love can lend itself to being shallow or unnecessarily self-indulgent (in the wrong hands), but with the right training, self-love can go bone-deep and genuinely transform you at a core level.

For those starting off on the inner work journey, I always recommend self-love as the best starting place. Without building a good relationship with yourself, the other forms of inner work explored in the next few points may be too intimidating, too hard, or plain old detrimental for your wellbeing.

Learning how to love yourself is absolutely imperative if you wish to find your soul mate or twin flame. As mentioned previously in this book, like attracts like. *We attract who we think we deserve.* When we carry the unconscious belief that we're ugly, stupid, unworthy, and unlovable, we will naturally gravitate toward those who reinforce this idea. As crazy as it may sound, the ego doesn't like to be wrong! Even if a person is clearly toxic and disturbed, the ego (as a way to try and protect the beliefs we have about who we are) will be drawn to those who confirm what we believe about ourselves deep down.

Self-love is a journey, not a destination. There is always more to love, more to forgive, and more to feel compassion for within ourselves. As with all forms of inner work, it's best to start small, but be consistent. Something as simple as choosing to eat food that is nourishing is a great start. Other excellent self-love practices include:

- Creating strong interpersonal boundaries
- Learning how to say no
- Standing up for yourself
- Valuing your needs and desires
- Pursuing your dreams
- Cutting away toxic people from your life
- Exploring your core beliefs
- Learning how to be your own best friend

One of my favorite forms of self-love is mirror work. Quite literally, mirror work involves using any mirror in your house to see your insecurities and fears clearly – but the focus isn't on the outside but on examining the *inside* of yourself. Mirror work also connects you with the deeper essence of who you truly are: the place that is full of profound compassion, self-acceptance, and forgiveness ... your soul.

To practice mirror work, stand in front of a mirror in private. Set aside about five to ten minutes. As you gaze into your eyes, begin to say kind things to yourself. You can do this out loud or in your mind. For instance, you might choose to say, "I love and forgive you, [insert name]." Using your name will increase the power of your affirmations. It's normal to feel a bit skeptical or judgmental toward yourself when first starting this practice. But keep persisting. If you get emotional at any point, give yourself a tender hug. You might also like to record your thoughts, feelings, and observations in a journal after this exercise.

Practice 5: Inner child work

One level deeper from self-love is inner child work, a form of inner work that involves examining your childhood wounds, fears, and beliefs.

To differing degrees, we all carry a wounded inner child. Our job as adults is to reconnect with this childlike part of ourselves, excavate old limiting childhood beliefs/fears, and integrate this delicate part of ourselves back into our waking consciousness.

Your inner child is a source of tremendous creativity, joy, spontaneity, love, and wisdom. However, at the same time, your inner child can also be a source of illogical obsessions, unshakable fears, neuroses, self-sabotaging behaviors, and limiting self-beliefs. It is these wounds that have a tremendously negative impact on relationships and your capacity to enjoy soul mate and twin flame relationships. By working to heal these wounds, we make ourselves more open to enjoying deep, mature and fulfilling love.

It must be stated clearly here that inner child work can rile up a lot of unfinished business. If you had an abusive childhood, you may feel a sense of disgust or looming fear towards this work (many do) or even toward your inner child. But as one who had an abusive childhood and who has done a lot of inner child work, I can tell you it is absolutely worth all of the pain, tears, and anger. You need to purge that crap and not let it control you! However, if at any point you feel overwhelmed, please stop immediately and practice self-care. If you find inner child work too challenging to do by yourself, you may need the help of a trained therapist. (After all, there is only so much we can do alone.)

One great way to work with your inner child is through journaling. Having a back-and-forth dialogue with your inner child can prove to be immensely illuminating. Doing inner child meditations and visualizations are also other beautiful ways to reconnect with this vulnerable part of you. I also find that creating art is a powerful way to harness the inner child's innate creativity and process intense emotions such as rage, grief, and fear.

Practice 6: Shadow work

At the deepest level of the inner work process is shadow work. This form of inner work is the most complex, elusive, and intimidating of all. With shadow work, we are literally exploring the shadowy places hidden within our psyches that we deliberately suppress, deny, and disown each and every day. And we all know what lurks in the shadows: the spine-chilling stuff of nightmares.

Shadow work is the practice of exploring your inner demons. Within your shadow lurks everything that has been outlawed, deemed 'taboo,' 'bad,' ugly, and unacceptable by your parents and society. It is this 'shadow self' that contains all the things you are secretly ashamed about and disgusted by within yourself. It is also your shadow self that contains the key to your emotional, psychological, and spiritual freedom. In fact, not only does exploring your shadow self produce such profound inner changes, but as a natural consequence, it upgrades your relationships to higher and purer levels of being as well.

At the root of all relationship struggles are unresolved shadow issues. That's it. If you keep sabotaging your chances of happiness with other people, that's your shadow. If you are addicted to codependent relationships, that's your shadow. If you're too emotionally unstable to hold down a healthy relationship, that's your shadow.

We are not our shadow, but our shadow *is* a part of us. We must come to terms with this reality and seek to understand, forgive, integrate, and transmute this part of ourselves. When we do, we feel a growing sense of joy, love, purpose, and expansion. In the context of twin flame and soul mate relationships, we can experience a state of Divine Union (such as is illustrated in ancient spiritual texts) that not only dramatically transforms us but also the world around us.

However, before attempting shadow work, it is absolutely imperative that you practice self-love. You must have stable and healthy self-esteem before doing shadow work. *"Why?"* you may wonder. Shadow work can easily make you feel a thousand times worse about yourself if you already have poor self-worth. For this reason, shadow work is an advanced form of inner work that is not for beginners. If you want to do shadow work, please explore self-love and inner child work beforehand.

If you feel prepared to begin shadow work, the best place to start is with the mirror work technique mentioned above. Instead of saying affirmations, simply stand in front of the mirror and gaze into your eyes. Try to keep your body relaxed. Then, observe what thoughts and feelings arise about yourself. The beautiful simplicity of this method is that the mirror shows us what is happening, regardless of whether we like it or not. The mirror, in essence, is a vessel of truth. For instance, if, on a deeply unconscious level, you feel ashamed or angry about who you are, those emotions will arise as you gaze at yourself. If you are burying away grief, those feelings will emerge. If you believe you're defective, lost, unwanted, or worthless, those thoughts will arise. Please take care with this practice. It can get intense if you aren't grounded or prepared. Consider having some self-loving affirmations on hand to help counteract any overwhelming negativity you may feel.

Once you have finished the mirror exercise, record your thoughts, feelings, and observations in a journal. In fact, having a journal for shadow work is essential. If you would like to start shadow work, buy yourself a paperback journal or sign up to an online note-taking platform like Evernote. If you would like a little bit of structure and guidance, Sol and I have created a Shadow Work Journal that you can use to start your journey. We've devised over sixty questions in this journal, each question opening a 'forbidden' doorway into the darker corners of the mind. Please see the references section at the end of this book for more information on where to find the Shadow Work Journal (if you would like to begin this work).

Above all, go slowly with shadow work. If at any time you feel overwhelmed, please stop immediately. Take time to ground yourself, practice self-care, and do a self-loving activity. Shadow work is one of the most powerful ways to help you find and thrive in a loving soul mate or twin flame relationship. But it should be approached with care and mindfulness.

Finding Love Requires Work

In this chapter, we've explored the biggest blocks to finding love, as well as six ways to overcome those constraints. What I want to emphasize here is that finding love, as much as we'd like to believe, does not always come easily. You can't always wish yourself towards finding your soul mate or twin flame. Sometimes Life surprises us out of the blue, but often it doesn't. Often we must intentionally work on ourselves and earn the right to be in a deeply fulfilling relationship. Why? The answer is that doing the work is part of the spiritual path. In reality, finding love is not separate from spiritually evolving and maturing: they are often one and the same journey. By doing the work, we are expressing our sincerity, courage, and devotion to improving ourselves, and therefore the world around us.

In actuality, this journey doesn't just benefit us: it helps others as well. The ego likes to think egocentrically – that finding love is all about us. But in reality, when we are on the journey to finding love, we are not only on the journey of finding ourselves, but also blessing the world with our discoveries. The more capacity we have to love ourselves and our partner, the more capacity we have to emanate love into the world around us. That, in truth, is why finding love can often be such a hard, but a profoundly worthy path.

In the next chapter, we'll explore some of the major destructive myths that surround soul mate and twin flame relationships. Often, these corrupting beliefs get in the way of finding and experiencing true and authentic love. Let's stop these myths from undermining us and our relationships once and for all.

"I believe my twin flame doesn't know that she's my flame. I'm wondering how I can get her back on track on our twin flame journey or even force her to awaken? I know we're destined to be together forever."

– Carlos (shared on social media)

CHAPTER 6

Harmful Myths About Twin Flame and Soul Mate Relationships

When we were young, we listened to mesmerizing stories about princes and princesses falling in love and getting married. We were taught that we only have one true love out there and that this person (who is always the opposite gender) completes us.

As we grow older, many of us seek to fulfill this romantic ideal. Some of us spend years pining and searching for the "perfect" lover who can tick all the boxes and match all of our criteria. In fact, some of us even carry around a mental idea of what our soul mate and twin flame will look like, sound like, and behave like. Being a romantic soul myself, I always thought that my soul mate would be a rough, Australian country guy. Perhaps I was simply projecting my own disowned anima (divine masculine energy) outwards? Instead, I fell in love with a rebellious and mysterious South

American man – and oddly enough, this was a perfect fit for me!

But I'm not the only one who has experienced the push-and-pull between social conditioning and the heart's authentic desires. So many of us think we know what we want in a person, when in fact we don't. And sometimes, when someone not-quite-matching our description comes along, we shut ourselves off, missing the opportunity.

To those of us who have experienced severe emotional and mental wounding in our lives, soul mates and twin flames appear as a kind of holy mecca or "promised land." When we feel incomplete, lonely and disconnected from ourselves, the ideal of true love becomes a beacon of hope promising to save us. Soon we start sincerely believing that our beloved will "complete us," and thus make our lives meaningful again. Unfortunately, such a myth is destructive to our mental, emotional, and psychological well-being in the long term (we'll explore why soon).

To find and thrive in a deep, loving spiritual relationship, we need to strip back the layers of harmful myths that we've adopted throughout life. These harmful myths not only obscure our ability to see clearly, but they can also prevent us from getting into soul-nourishing relationships because we carry certain ideas and beliefs that aren't being appeased. In extreme circumstances, the myths we've inherited from our societies can actually undermine and destroy our relationships from the inside out. This is tragic but very real – and sadly quite common.

In this chapter, we'll explore the core soul mate and twin flame myths you need to be aware of to protect yourself and enjoy the love that is your birthright to experience. First, we'll start with the major soul mate myths and follow that with the central twin flame myths. Get ready to have some of those ingrained beliefs challenged!

Soul Mate Love Myths

Deep down many of us believe that there is at least one person out there who will fulfill all of our needs and desires. In fact, such a warped belief is what causes such high divorce rates and relationship dysfunction running rife in our societies.

There are so many harmful myths about soul mates that circulate through our cultural dialogues. These myths end up as rigid stories and ideals that play on repeat within our minds. In fact, these ideals and beliefs are directly responsible for limiting our spiritual growth and capacity to mature as divine beings. Believing that anything outside of yourself will complete or make you whole is not only misguided, but highly dangerous to your spiritual, emotional, and psychological well-being.

So with this in mind, let's explore ten of the most common soul mate love myths out there:

Myth 1. You can control when and where you meet your soul mate

First of all, it's important to drop the illusion of control. When it comes to finding true love, all you can really do is be open and receptive to meeting your soul mate and do the inner work. The human ego tends to believe that it can control life. But life can't be controlled. Life is just as wise, wild and mysterious as it is frustrating! Our soul mates often appear "out of the blue" when we least expect them to. But it's also quite common to intuit, sense or dream about your soul mate before they suddenly appear in your life.

Myth 2. What you want in your soul mate is what you'll get

We tend to approach relationships with preconceived notions of what we want or need. So many articles out there that I've read recommend "visualizing your soul mate" so as to attract them into your life. However, this is another trick of the ego. The law of attraction doesn't quite work that way. It is your thoughts and beliefs that reflect your reality. Your soul mate often isn't someone you consciously desire, but someone you *unconsciously* attract and need for inner growth. While you can prime the mind with symbolic acts (such as rituals) to be open and receptive to finding your soul mate, you won't necessarily get the soul mate you envision – you'll get who you *need*.

Myth 3. Soul mates will stay with you no matter what

This is another highly harmful myth that creates a lot of unnecessary pain. As a species we find great comfort in the thought of "always and forever" (hence why marriage is so appealing to us). But this isn't always the case. Sometimes our soul mates stay for a season, and sometimes they stay for a lifetime. Whatever the case, the belief that our soul mates will stay with us forever is a recipe for complacency, stagnation, and severe heartbreak.

Myth 4. We only have *one* soul mate

This point is a matter of personal opinion. However, I believe it is possible to have more than one soul mate in a lifetime. Talking to many people about their thoughts and experiences on love, I've discovered that a great number have had "multiple" soul mate experiences. Each was different, precious and life-changing in varied ways. I do, however, believe that we only have one twin flame relationship.

Myth 5. Soul mates are always romantic/sexual

On the contrary, soul mate relationships can be completely platonic with no sexual or romantic feelings involved whatsoever. In other words, your soul mate could simply be your best friend in the world.

Myth 6. Soul mates are human

We think of soul mates in terms of humans loving other humans. But many people have felt intense and strong bonds with landforms, animals, and pets that transcend human language.

Myth 7. Soul mates are the opposite gender

Religion and tradition would have us believe that soul mates are heterosexual in nature. In reality, love is free: it is not restricted by what is dogmatically judged as "right" or "wrong." Your soul mate could very well be of the same gender as you. If you identify as heterosexual, this will obviously come as a great shock to you. However, it will ultimately encourage you to reclaim your authentic sexuality.

Myth 8. Soul mates are single

Love is a complex emotion. It is true that "we can't choose who we love" — love flows freely and runs wild. Who can claim to understand the mysteries of the heart? As such, many people are tormented by the fact that the one they love is already in a relationship or marriage. This is not the same as seeking exciting lust-filled escapades out of boredom: soul mates resonate much deeper than great chemistry, sex, or compatible interests. When soul mates are in this tough position, they must choose to move on or break up their marriage. There is, of course, a third option, secretive infidelity, but that will inevitably result in great suffering for all parties involved, so isn't obviously advised. While choosing to move on or choosing to stay are painful in their own ways, both decisions are ultimately catalysts for enormous emotional and spiritual growth.

Myth 9. Soul mate relationships are effortless

There is a widespread assumption that soul mate love is easy and stress-free. This belief adds to the desirability and idealization of such a relationship. However, soul mate relationships require time, effort, patience and diligence like any other relationships. Without conscious maintenance, even soul mate relationships will fail.

Myth 10. Soul mates make you whole

This is perhaps the most destructive myth of all. The belief that our soul mates make us whole is not only misleading, but it is also highly self-disrespecting. We are taught to believe that our soul mates are our "missing halves" when in fact they are helpers and catalysts of our spiritual growth. The belief that our soul mate "makes us whole" is so popular because it encourages us to bypass responsibility for our happiness and wholeness. It's much easier to put the burden and pressure on others! So many people enter relationships believing their soul mate will give them everything they need. This, unfortunately, leads to issues such as codependency, toxic enabling, and self-betrayal.

Instead of looking outside for completion, why not look inside of your own precious and unexplored soul? Everything — all the love, acceptance and joy you need — is waiting there to be found.

Twin Flame Love Myths

We'll now move onto some key twin flame love myths that you need to be aware of.

As we've already explored, twin flame relationships are among some of the most potent connections of life – and they are increasing at an unprecedented rate.

Gone are the days of mating for power, royal influence, practicality and religious jurisdiction. Now, more than ever, we are free to meet and greet who we like, comb through thousands of possible suitors on the internet, and commit when we are ready. When else in history have we been granted such freedom?

But with this newfound freedom also comes the potential for immense growth both psychologically and spiritually. This is where twin flames come into the picture. What is so striking about twin flame relationships is that they are cataclysmic in their ability to revolutionize our lives, just as an earthquake is cataclysmic in its potential to transform any landscape.

Because of their sheer power and breathtaking catalytic nature, twin flame relationships are often romanticized, idealized and worshiped in unnecessary and misguided ways just as the false idol is lauded for its imaginary divinity. While the connections that twin flames have are indeed divine, they are also intensely unsettling and overburdened with dense layers of limiting myths.

7 Misconceptions About Twin Flame Relationships

The role of the twin flame is to aid you in the development of inner wholeness, harmony, and self-realization (Oneness) – but this journey certainly isn't full of sunshine and roses. In fact, the meeting of two twin flames is like the meeting of the sun and moon, earth and sky, fire and water: both partners mirror precisely what the other lacks. Understandably this can create divine harmony, but also intense conflict within a relationship.

So what are the most common myths and misconceptions about twin flame relationships? And furthermore, what can you expect if you have truly met your soul's mirror? We'll explore that below:

Myth 1 – Your twin flame completes you.

Reality – Your twin flame helps you to become more complete. They don't complete you.

It sounds so beautiful to "be completed" by another person, and on one level this is true of twin flames. Twin flames complete us in the sense that they serve as the catalysts to our wholeness. In other words, our twin flames reveal to us what areas we are lacking (in my case it was humility, open-mindedness, and compassion). However, our twin flames in and of themselves do not complete us. They are *not* our "other halves." Why? Because beneath all the layers of beliefs, wounds, conditioning, and ego-masks lie pure and infinite perfection. How can pure and infinite perfection ever be incomplete? It's the ego/mind that thinks it is incomplete, but the soul knows otherwise. And that is the role of our twin flames; to remind us of the truth of who we are, that our souls are Whole.

Myth 2 – Your twin flame is a member of the opposite sex.

Reality – Your twin flame might be the same gender as you.

The heterosexual ideal still permeates a lot of twin flame literature. But life doesn't adhere to traditional thought, religious influence, or even the gender binary system. In reality, your twin flame could be the same sex as you, which might cause you to question your sexuality and other beliefs about life.

Myth 3 – Your twin flame is just like you.

Reality – Your twin flame is most likely your "opposite."

Although you both share many similarities, you also share a surprising number of differences. However, these differences deeply contribute to the relationship rather than taking away from it. For example, while you might be an introvert, your partner might be more outgoing. While they might be more masculine, you might be more feminine. And you will both share opposing strengths and weaknesses, e.g., you might be more sensitive, they might be more rough-around-the-edges; you might be impulsive, they might be sensible; you might be calm, they might be anxious, and so forth. Essentially, you are both the embodiment of the "yin and yang."

Myth 4 – Your twin flame will come at the right time and be in the right place.

Reality – Your twin flame might appear at the worst possible time.

Or, they might appear at the best possible time. Life isn't always predictable. For instance, you might meet your twin flame but discover that they are already married. Or you might connect with your twin flame at a bad time (e.g., during or after a crisis). There is no set rule.

Myth 5 – You will always recognize your twin flame straight away.

Reality – You might not initially recognize your twin flame until much later in life.

We are all at different levels, or stages, of conscious development in life. Sol and I refer to this as *soulful or spiritual maturity* and speak about this in terms of soul ages (which symbolize the various psychospiritual 'stages' we inhabit on our paths to Wholeness). For example, 'younger souls' will have a much harder time distinguishing their twin flames from everyday lovers – until they realize that no matter how far they travel, they will keep returning back to their flames. 'Older souls,' on the other hand, will have a much easier time recognizing their twin flames, but might also be subject to romanticizing or idealizing the connection, resulting in a lot of frustration.

Myth 6 – You can force your twin flame to awaken.

Reality – Your twin flame will awaken when their soul is ready.

Trying to force your twin flame to awaken is like trying to get a plant to grow by digging it out of the ground. Everything takes time, and while that can be extremely frustrating to come to terms with, it's not our place to try and "force" awakening upon our flames. Not only is it largely a waste of energy (as the more we push, the more our partners will likely resist us out of fear), but it is also disrespectful. We need to understand that all souls are different and by pressuring them to prematurely awaken there could be tremendously negative side effects – for both of you. So give them space. Lead by example. In their own time, they will awaken.

Myth 7 – Twin flame relationships are always happy, smiley, and perfect.

Reality – Twin flame relationships can be tumultuous, overwhelming, and intense.

Ideally, twin flame relationships flourish into wonderfully harmonious spaces full of joy, peace, love, understanding, and spiritual expansion. While these qualities do define twin flame relationships after many years of inner work, they don't always. In fact, in the beginning, twin flame relationships can be riddled with the most intense arguments and clashes conceivable (however, please don't mistake this as flat out abuse – please see the next chapter for an in-depth look at this distinction). Many people refer to this as "karmic cleansing" where all our faults, flaws, and deepest core wounds are brought to the light to be dealt with and healed. Of course, this can be extremely disturbing, particularly when two big egos are involved in maintaining their illusion of greatness.

The tricky thing is, our flames know what buttons to push, and how to stir up and provoke our greatest fears, shames, and secrets like no one has ever done before. This is usually not done with malicious intent (and if it is, be careful and reassess the relationship!), but unconsciously and automatically, resulting in more profound internal growth. Eventually, both partners will be able to empathetically understand each other at a core level and continue their dual quest for self-realization.

Myth 8 – You'll immediately be ready to invite your twin flame into your life.

Reality – You might not be ready to open up to your twin flame.

As I mentioned before, our twin flames don't always arise at the right time and place in our lives. In my own case, I was still in the depths of religious conditioning and dogma when I met Sol, so it took me many months before I could realize the true, deep significance of the connection. In your own case, it might take many months, even years to truly fathom the significance of your twin flame who may or may not play an active role in your life. Due to the intensity of twin flame relationships, it is common for the connection to disintegrate very quickly and later re-emerge in life when both partners are emotionally, mentally and spiritually ready.

Question Everything

Yes, even what I have written above. Don't believe anything unless it makes emotional and rational sense to *you*. No matter how big an 'expert' someone is, don't buy into what they say, especially if it makes you feel unworthy, lacking, or somehow in desperate need. There are many sharks out there in the proverbial fish tank of life who will seek to sell you a version of *their* truth, without making space for you to honor yours. So please, honor your truth. Don't accept the endless array of love myths out there that are used to prey on your vulnerabilities. Question everything people tell you about soul mates and twin flames, and only accept what is true for you on a core soul level. You will know it's true when it makes you feel expansive, empowered, and serene inside.

In the next chapter, we'll explore the different levels of romantic connection, and how this hierarchy of needs forms the underlying skeleton of soul mate and twin flame relationships. Not only must we be aware of the toxic external myths that threaten to overrun our love lives, but we must also see our relationships from an objective, bird's-eye perspective to create more balance and harmony. If you're wanting to create a stable, strong, long-lasting relationship that is fulfilling on every level, the next chapter will be vital for you to read.

To love is to be in communion with the other

and to discover in that other the spark of God.

– Paulo Coelho

CHAPTER 7

The Five Levels of Relationships

Our relationships reflect the seasons, elements, and cycles of life. They are multi-faceted in nature and rarely stay the same. In fact, if they *don't* evolve, that is a big warning sign as stagnation and decay have set in. Flux and change is a good thing. It is normal and healthy for every relationship to ebb and flow to the rhythms of our inner and outer worlds.

In this chapter we'll briefly cover the five levels of relationships and why they're essential to comprehend if we're to thrive in stable and long-lasting soul mate and twin flame partnerships. Keep in mind that while we'll be discussing "levels," this process is not linear. In other words, we rarely move from point A to point Z. Instead, we often move through these levels in a messy, overlapping, and zigzagged way.

What are the five levels? In his essay entitled *Conscious Love,* clinical psychologist John Welwood loosely defined them as:

1. Fusion (fire)
2. Companionship (earth)
3. Community (air)
4. Communication (water)
5. Communion (spirit)

You'll notice that one of the five elements has been placed next to each level. This is a unique addition I've added to help you get a clear 'feel' of each level and its significance. (If you're not familiar with the five elements and what they represent, fire symbolizes passion and dynamism, earth symbolizes practicality and the material world, air symbolizes the mind, water symbolizes the heart, spirit symbolizes the spiritual dimension.)

As we'll see, love is like an ever-expanding circle, and the closer we reach to level five (communion) the more nourishing on a personal level and deeply fulfilling on a universal level our relationships will be.

Below we'll look at each level more in-depth:

Level 1: Fusion (fire)

The most basic, primitive level of twin flame and soul mate relationships is the urge to bond through *symbiotic fusion.* In this level, we seek to obtain the emotional nourishment that we lacked as children within the space of our new relationship. It's common for couples (or even friends) who enter this stage to want to do *everything* together. In the process, they'll often ignore other relationships in their lives and dedicate most of their free time to their partners.

The fusion level, which is at the very heart of all 'whirlwind romances' and blissful, passionate, and dreamlike rendezvous, helps to establish close emotional bonding. But while it's an important initial level, if it goes on for too long (i.e., around two or more years), it can become a form of addiction and confines the growth of both individuals.

Level 2: Companionship (earth)

The need for companionship, or basic friendship, is the next level. In this level, both partners learn to share each other's space and company. It is in this level where "trouble in paradise" starts as practical reality sets in, often with a big wake-up slap across the face. No longer is the relationship solely about the intense and ecstatic bliss of two souls reuniting, but it's also about *grounding that connection in reality.*

Unfortunately, not all couples can withstand this level. If they came to see the fusion stage and its blissful nature as the baseline against which to compare the *rest* of the relationship, there is trouble. The realities of life can become too hard to bear for couples who carry too much dreamlike idealism. Sadly, the result is that many relationships crumble in this level. Sometimes heaven cannot tolerate earth.

However, those who learn to be not just passionate lovers, but also solid friends, will be rewarded tremendously in the future levels. But first, the daily monotony, and stark flaws and ugly habits of the other must be embraced.

Level 3: Community (air)

Companionship becomes *community* in a relationship when both partners can relate to each other on the level of the mind, not just day-to-day earthly matters. When soul mates and twin flames live in a community together, they share the same interests, goals, and values. Most fundamentally, they are capable of carrying a shared vision together whether that be creating a beautiful garden, supporting a charity, raising conscious children, or fuelling a large-scale social/ecological/spiritual movement.

Level 4: Communication (water)

Sharing the same interests, goals, and values (as in the community level) cannot be complete without clear communication. Communication is the most crucial ingredient in the overall health and wellbeing of a relationship, but it's not as easy as it sounds. Certainly, it's easy to *talk* but much more challenging to *communicate*. The difference between the two is that talking is merely vomiting out our thoughts and feelings, whereas communication is mindfully sharing what we carry within us with emotional intelligence and sensitivity.

When a soul mate or twin flame couple merely talk to each other, issues in misunderstanding and misinterpretation always arise. But when a soul mate or twin flame couple communicate their deepest thoughts, feelings, dreams, and desires from a place of mutual receptivity, there is clarity, compassion, and understanding.

What is mutual receptivity? This is a term that refers to the ability to be open and sensitive to both *our* needs and our partner's needs. Being receptive requires practice, the development of good listening skills, and the ability to be honest and clear about what we think and feel. Ultimately, however, clear communication requires courage – the courage to truly be seen, heard, and understood, and also the courage to do likewise for our partners. We need to be able to honor the different backgrounds, perceptions, feelings, and truths existing within our relationships, and this can take time.

Level 5: Communion (spirit)

The final level is communion which is a rare level that cannot be 'achieved' so much as it can be spontaneously experienced. Communion is a gift from Life itself. It exists in those moments when we are walking in the woods, making love, looking into our partner's eyes, and listening to a beautiful song together. In these moments, time stands still, and there is a full and holy recognition of the other Soul before us. At times, this experience of deep communion with the other can give way to mystical experiences of complete Oneness and Union. But usually, there is an unspoken feeling of being truly seen and loved for who we are at a core level.

Those who have experienced such a deep and profound communion with their partners may often desire to merge into One awakened being. But as we can see in tragic archetypal stories such as Romeo and Juliet and Tristan and Isolde, wanting our relationships to fulfill this spiritually elevated role leads to tremendous suffering. As Welwood puts it, "Putting our whole longing for spiritual realization onto a finite relationship can lead to idealization, inflation, addiction, and death. The most appropriate way to address our longing for union is through a genuine spiritual practice." This is the biggest trap inherent in level five: we can get lost in trying to deify our relationship to its own destruction. As we reiterate over and over again in this book, it is not our twin flame or soul mate that makes us whole. We are innately whole at our core. Our twin flames and soul mates are spiritual catalysts that help us to grow and transform on every level. Trying to merge with or use our partners to "become complete" is a recipe for pain and quite literally the annihilation of our relationship.

The solution to trying to merge into One is to be both separate and together, distinct but unified at the same time. The soul mates and twin flames who make the biggest impact within this world (and who are the happiest) are those who honor and respect the boundaries of individuality but also strive for unification and the sacred marriage of opposites. Ultimately, we can see the pinnacle of mature soul mate and twin flame love in the image of the yin and yang: two circles of distinctly different colors existing within one larger circle.

In chapter 11 we'll go more into depth on how to create this divine balance. But first, let's actively explore your relationship. How healthy is it? What are some warning signs you need to be aware of? Now that you have the big picture perspective (presented in the five stages above) let's explore how to get to the communion stage by exploring the inner demons that arise within our soul mate and twin flame relationships.

"I think my soul mate is an energy vampire. I keep running away from him due to being triggered, which I never blame him for. But it feels like my worst life drama is playing out as he's using his love to manipulate me. He becomes more and more distant and I have to give an increasing amount of my energy to ensure he doesn't leave me. I give lots of energy and get very little in return. This is having a horrendous psychological effect on me ..."

– ANAYA (shared via email)

CHAPTER 8

Are You in a Healthy Relationship?

Although we'd like to believe it, not all soul mate and twin flame relationships are healthy. If they were perfectly healthy all the time, there would be no opportunity for growth and transformation.

But don't mistake normal unhealthiness (stemming from core wounds and insecurities) with pathological toxicity. There is a big difference between 'normal' dysfunction in a relationship and flat out abuse. Unfortunately, many people justify abusive behavior in their "twin flame" or "soul mate" relationships believing that it's somehow their destiny to fix or "save" their partner who is simultaneously traumatizing them. But it is *not* our responsibility to fix or save our partners – that is *their* responsibility and karmic duty, not ours. (See Appendix 1 for a lengthier exploration of the topic of self-responsibility in soul mate and twin flame relationships.)

In this chapter, we'll explore the fundamental difference between healthy and unhealthy spiritual partnerships. As the following information will take a certain level of introspection and reflection, I encourage you to go slowly. You might even like to journal about your thoughts and discuss them with your partner (if you have one right now).

Signs of a Healthy Relationship

> *A no-effort relationship is a doomed relationship, not a great relationship. It takes work to communicate accurately and it takes work to expose and resolve conflicting hopes and beliefs. It doesn't mean there is no "they lived happily ever after," but it's more like "they worked happily ever after.*

– CAROL DWECK

All soul mate and twin flame relationships are unique, complex, and multi-layered. However, there are some key defining characteristics that all healthy couples share. Here they are:

1. You are both equals

Even though you have fights and slip-ups, you are still both equals in the relationship. You don't feel superior to your partner, and your partner doesn't feel elevated above or "better than" you: you are both on the same page, even though that page may be riddled with scribbles and tears.

2. You are both willing to compromise in healthy ways

There isn't just one person in your partnership constantly sacrificing their desires or preferences; both of you are willing to compromise in ways that benefit both of you.

3. You are *heard*, not just listened to

There is a difference between hearing and listening: *hearing* is the process of actively understanding what a person is telling you and getting involved, and *listening* is the process of allowing words to enter your ears, but not necessarily emotionally or mentally contributing. When you hear your partner, and your partner hears you, there is a mutual bond of respect. However, when one partner only listens, and the other partner hears (or worse, both partners only listen), there is an immense imbalance, and likely a loss of respect.

4. You both try your best to resolve conflicts

Even though you might not be the best at communicating or the best at making up, you always try your best to resolve conflicts – as does your partner. You might shout, scream, or make a fuss at each other, but at the end of the day, you try to move past your differences and agree to disagree. However, one sign of a toxic, unhealthy relationship is dragging past conflicts into the present. When one (or both) partners "keep a count" of all the wrongdoings the other has inflicted on them, this is a red flag. When conflicts are drawn out, this is a sign that there are underlying threads of bitterness and contempt in one or both partners that springs from a lack of forgiveness. If left unchecked, this can evolve into deep resentment.

5. You celebrate each other's achievements

If you succeed, achieve or win something, your partner is quick to congratulate you and celebrate alongside you – and vice versa. However, one sign of an unhealthy relationship is withholding your happiness for your partner's achievements, and instead criticizing them, belittling them, "one-upping" them, or returning mock enthusiasm. If you experience this (or give this) in your relationship, consider it a red flag.

6. You both freely give affection to each other

Affection in your relationship is freely given spontaneously. Affection isn't doled out in small measured portions, or used as a bargaining chip (i.e., "I'll offer sex if you do this for me"), or otherwise used to manipulate or control each other. Affection is the sacred glue that binds you both together.

7. You can be honest with your partner

You don't fear your partner, and your partner doesn't fear you; instead, you both feel comfortable enough to be honest, forthcoming and transparent with each other. Even though your partner might get angry at you (or you at your partner), you can nevertheless give and receive the truth openly among each other. Punishment in the form of silent treatment, emotional blackmail, or physical harm is a major red flag. Secrecy is also another glaring sign of an unhealthy relationship.

8. Authenticity is encouraged in your relationship

Both of you can be genuine and authentic, and openly pursue what you love without hindrances of any kind. If you feel as though you have a lot of space to grow in your relationship, this is a good sign. However, if you feel smothered, controlled, repressed or barred-in, this is a bad sign.

9. You both invite growth and change

Although you both might hate to admit your flaws and weaknesses, you're both open to growing and changing as people. However, if one or both partners stubbornly refuses to grow, this is a seriously unhealthy sign. Also, if your partner is forcing you to change (and vice versa), this is a red flag as well.

10. You share the same life goals and values with each other

How stable is the foundation on which your relationship is built? Is it built on superficial tastes, likes, or personality characteristics? Or is it built on a deeper foundation of shared values, goals, and beliefs? Your answer to this question will determine the depth, compatibility, and potential for long-term growth your relationship has. Healthy relationships are built on shared life goals and values.

As I mentioned previously, no relationship is perfect. Imperfection will always, to some extent, be present within your relationship. So it's normal for a few issues to emerge (like poor communication, selfishness, etc.). When Luna and I first got together, we had many fights arising from our opposing perspectives of the world and different upbringings. And although we've grown past that tumultuous period, we do have arguments every now and then stemming from petty misunderstandings, miscommunications, and general grouchiness. So again, no relationship is sunshine and roses all the time.

However, it's essential to be aware when a certain pattern of behavior moves into the 'red flag' zone – as in, it starts becoming destructive and crippling to the health and very foundation of the relationship. When worst comes to worst, it's important to (a) reassess the nature of your relationship (i.e., is it a true soul mate or twin flame connection?) and (b) take decisive action, whether that be to try and salvage the relationship or move on from it. We'll explore how to make these tough decisions later in the chapter, but first, let's examine the four major issues underlying most relationship problems.

Why Are Relationships So Hard, Frustrating, and Painful?

This is a question most of us wonder at some point: *why are relationships so damn complicated?* Why can't we just experience harmonious union all the time without the suffering? Thankfully, with a bit of self-education, we can understand why it's so hard for us to maintain healthy relationships.

Here are the top four reasons why our relationships suffer. Keep in mind that what is written below applies to *both sides* (i.e., you *and* your partner):

1. We impose our desires, expectations, and beliefs onto our partners

When we are continually forcing our partner to be anything other than what they *authentically are* we create an immense amount of tension in our relationships. Essentially we are saying to them, "You are not good enough as you are and you better change, or I won't love you." Mostly we are unaware of our tendency to force our stories down our partner's throats, and so we wind up in endless circuses of drama.

Examples of desires, expectations, and beliefs that we unconsciously adopt include, for instance, "You *should* do this or else …" "You *should* behave like this because …" "You *shouldn't* do that …" "You *have to* like/dislike this …"

What can we do in such a situation? The solution is to explore the ways you force your desires, expectations, and beliefs onto your partner (or how they do it to you). You will be able to tell by the feeling of tension (resistance) that arises in your body. Once you've done the hard work of exploring the unspoken rules dragging down your relationship, you can work on mutually satisfying compromises.

2. We struggle to communicate openly and honestly (without repercussion)

The number one mistake most of us make in our relationships is our inability to communicate openly. Because of our fear and insecurity, most of us clamp up and interact in a vague, ambiguous way to avoid clashes. And even if we *do* courageously venture to tell the truth to our partners, we are often met with anger, emotional blackmail, and even open hostility.

What's the solution in this situation? The best thing you can do is explore the topic of communication. Think about the following questions:

- Can you communicate clearly and honestly about what you do/don't like in your relationship?
- Can you communicate freely without condemnation or rejection?
- Do you struggle to be assertive (or does your partner)?

If you answer yes to any of these three questions, there isn't enough open communication in your relationship. You'll need to work together to create a 'safe place' in which both of you strive to maintain open minds and compassionate hearts. Without the freedom to be honest and transparent with each other, your relationship will always suffer. It will be worth investing time in learning healthy communication skills either via a book, course or therapist. (Please see the Bibliography section if you need more resources.)

3. We project our childhood traumas onto our partners

Unconsciously projecting our childhood traumas onto our partners is a big reason why our relationships can become painful and difficult to maintain. Unfortunately, these traumas usually set the tone for how we perceive ourselves, others, and the world at large later in life. For instance, if I grew up with an emotionally cold and distant mother, it is likely that in later life I would seek a partner that fills that void, e.g., a partner who is overly possessive, controlling and smothering with affection. Or else I might attract the same type of woman (cold and distant) who I unconsciously seek to "right wrongs" with and win the affection of in an attempt to soothe my core wound of feeling "unlovable."

When we project our childhood traumas onto our partners, we are essentially using them as a way of trying to meet our unmet needs. Not only do we fail to see our partner accurately for who they *truly* are, but we superimpose a story on top of them that we cling on to. Can you imagine how frustrating and destructive that would be in a relationship? Usually, both partners are projecting their issues onto each other, and so they can never relate to each other on an authentic, mature level.

What can we do in this situation? The best approach to take is to do inner work (self-love, inner child work, shadow work) and possibly relationship counseling or personal therapy. You'll need to be able to clearly identify the core wounds driving your behavior (along with your partner) to prevent projection from occurring. While this may sound simple, it can be quite a difficult process as our traumas are coupled with an immense amount of pain, grief, and anger. This work takes time and effort, but it is worth every second.

4. We lack authentic self-love

The final major reason why our relationships can feel so hard, frustrating, and painful is that we lack self-love. Have you ever wondered why the love we experience in relationships can feel so conditional and so fleeting? There's a reason why, and that is because when we don't know how to love ourselves, we don't really know how to love others. As the famous saying by Jesus goes, "Love your neighbor as yourself." How can you love your neighbor if you don't know how first to love yourself? How can you give to another (i.e., your soul mate or twin flame) what *you* don't possess in the first place?

Self-love is a vital part of any relationship as it builds a foundation of authentic, healthy and pure love. Without self-love, our relationships are fueled by neediness, obsession, fear, jealousy, and pain. Without self-love, we will always be trying to steal from our partners what we lack inside (love). Without self-love, we will always be motivated by painful, unfulfilled needs. But with self-love, we are no longer motivated by anything other than the desire to give love because we already have everything we need – from ourselves.

What can we do if our issue is a lack of self-love? Obviously, the answer is to learn how to love ourselves more. But the problem is that we're conditioned to believe that self-love is "selfish" and self-sacrifice is "noble." Please understand that self-love does not mean being narcissistic or self-absorbed. Instead, it refers to developing profound inner compassion, acceptance, and understanding for yourself. In order to develop self-love, you'll need to dismantle the unhealthy narrative surrounding self-love and see how it undermines your behavior. It will also be worth examining the idea of self-sacrifice (which comes from a place of inner lack) and compassion (which comes from a place of inner fullness).

What to Do When Your Partner Isn't On the Spiritual Path

There's another reason why our relationships can become hard, frustrating, and painful, and that is a difference in belief.

You might meditate, practice mindfulness, do inner child work, shadow work, burn incense, communicate with your spirit guides and passionately commit yourself to a spiritual path … but the only problem is that your soul mate or twin flame may not be on the same page as you. They may not be interested in spirituality. In fact, not only might they *not* be interested in the spiritual path but they might also have a hard time understanding *why* you engage in various spiritual practices in the first place.

You may have thought to yourself, "can this relationship survive?" This is a troubling thought and may be accompanied by feelings of anxiety, emotional discomfort or even a sensation of looming endangerment. Is your relationship doomed if it isn't "spiritual"? This is a complex topic that we'll explore in this section.

Does Your Relationship Encourage Spiritual Growth?

I'll say it before, and I'll say it again: there's no such thing as a cookie cutter twin flame or soul mate relationship. All relationships are beautiful and unique in their own way. So does your partner need to have the same beliefs or spiritual path as you? No. It's not always essential.

But even though it's not always essential to have a partner who's interested in spirituality, it *is* essential to have a partnership that encourages spiritual growth. When relationships create an openly (or subtly) hostile atmosphere toward any form of inner transformation, the result is a toxic and stagnant environment.

Here are eight major red flags to look out for inherent in relationships that don't promote spiritual growth:

- Your partner makes fun of you and your practice
- Your partner gets angry when you dedicate time to your spirituality
- Your partner tries to prevent you from practicing your spiritual path
- Your partner has created a spoken or unspoken "ultimatum," i.e., "it's me or your spirituality"

- Your partner frequently criticizes your spiritual beliefs
- You feel the need to "hide" your spiritual practice and do it in secret
- You feel pressured to believe/follow what your partner believes
- You're afraid of sharing your spirituality for fear of being judged or rejected

If you can relate to two or more of these red flags, you should be concerned. Your relationship is most likely oppressive and doesn't allow you to grow as a person which means that there is an *unhealthy dynamic* going on. I would advise you to spend some quiet time across the next few weeks reconsidering your relationship. Why? Because you have the right to practice whatever form of spirituality speaks to your soul. You have the right to flourish as a spiritual being and be loved and supported – not rejected or judged negatively.

If, however, you can't relate to the above red flags but your partner isn't spiritual, and you are, this is a positive sign (but also more complex). You'll need to deconstruct the societal beliefs you've inherited as well as your core needs to determine whether the relationship will truly nourish you or not. I'll explain why below.

Toxic Comparison and True Love

Understandably it can be frustrating and disheartening to live with (or spend a lot of time around) a person who doesn't share the same aspirations, outlooks, or spiritual beliefs as you.

But I want to mention something essential here: *beware of the ideals you create.*

Concepts such as having 'twin flames' and 'soul mates' can be useful in defining and understanding relationships, but they are ultimately limiting and constrictive when framed in the purely spiritual context. Yes, you can still have a "non-spiritual" soulmate or twin flame: they don't need to be spiritual. So if you are looking jealously at other couples who seem to "have it all" spiritually speaking, drop those rose-tinted glasses as soon as possible.

"Spiritual" relationships are not the be-all and end-all. In other words, *no* you don't have to be in a spiritual relationship to be happy. No, you don't need to share the same metaphysical beliefs or outlooks. However, it is important to share the same values (which are less cerebral and more emotional.)

Why is it not essential to share the same spiritual beliefs? The answer is that the most "spiritual" thing is ultimately *love.*

If we are talking about real spirituality here (not just the various methods, paths or mental beliefs out there), what ultimately matters is *how much you love and accept each other, regardless of your differences.*

Beware of the toxic comparison that makes you feel like you should both be on the same page about everything, like "other people." Beware of the toxic comparison that makes you feel like you should be posting pictures of yourself and your partner on Instagram doing something "spiritual" like yoga – or go on week-long meditation retreats together – like "other couples."

As a person who has written a lot on spiritual relationships I can tell you this: *If your partner can love, they are innately spiritual.* It doesn't matter *what* they believe (or don't believe) so long as they can open their heart to you.

So put your foot down and refuse to be pressured into believing that your relationship has to look or feel a certain way. Your relationship is unique, and so long as it is based on mutual love and respect, it is healthy and can most assuredly survive.

A Little Side Note on Core Needs

On a side note, I want to say that it *is* possible to have a healthy and loving relationship, but the connection still isn't right for you. Why may this be the case? The answer is that one of your core needs isn't being met. If you absolutely feel in your heart of hearts that you need a partner who is on the same page as you spiritually, that is one of your *core needs*. And you need to pay attention to it

There are no easy answers here, and all I can say is that if you are unhappy in your relationship *despite* the fact that it is loving and respectful, it may not be the right relationship for you.

Not everyone needs to be in a relationship with a spiritual person, but if you feel the deep core need to be, then you need to do some soul searching. Reflect on yourself and your relationship in five years: does the thought make you happy or does it make you feel restless/depressed? If you answered the latter, then it is unlikely your relationship will be able to survive simply because one of your core needs is to have a spiritual, romantic companion. And that's perfectly okay. You will need to sort out your feelings and plan for the best path of action. Give yourself some space and time to sort through how you feel and reach some clarity. You have the right to live a full life and thrive in a relationship that meets your deepest needs. And while this may create upset and temporary instability, your deeper and wiser self will thank you in the future.

How to Thrive in a Healthy Non-Spiritual Relationship

So now that we've cleared up whether a relationship can survive or not when one partner isn't spiritual, here are some ways to ensure that your relationship continues to flourish:

Don'ts:

1. **Don't pressure your partner** to adopt the same spiritual beliefs or practices as you – *they* must ultimately decide for themselves. So be cautious of trying to deprive them of that empowered choice no matter how zealous you feel. Honor their free will.

2. **Be careful of harboring negative judgment** or a critical attitude towards your partner just because they are different. Remember that we are *all* at

various levels of spiritual awakening. When the time comes (*if* it comes) your partner will awaken too.

3. **Don't get lost in rose-tinted ideals and fantasies** about who your partner "should" be spiritually speaking. Wanting or expecting your partner to be anything other than what they are is a recipe for disaster. Accept the full package of your partner (strengths and flaws alike).

4. **Don't rely exclusively on your partner for spiritual nourishment** – this point may seem obvious, but you'd be surprised by how many people out there expect their partners to be "all things and everything." Take that burden off your partner and find a local spiritual group (or at the very least, one online) where you can express the spiritual side of yourself.

Do's:

1. **Lead by example (don't preach to convert).** There is nothing as nauseating as a person trying to proselytize others – so don't be pushy with your beliefs and outlooks. Walk the talk instead. Put your spirituality into action and *live* it.

2. **Find and focus on the similarities** between you and your partner.//
3. **Regularly express your love, commitment, and affection** (which itself is a spiritual practice).
4. **See your relationship as a "school of life"** and your partner as a teacher in disguise. So much self-knowledge and spiritual growth can occur within relationships, regardless of how outwardly "spiritual" they are. Your partner will mirror your greatest hidden strengths and also your most feared shadows. So see your connection as sacred without being overbearing.
5. **Honor what stage your partner is at.** Be careful of seeing yourself as more spiritually "advanced" than your partner (which leads to an inflated ego) – choose to see the two of you at *different levels* on the spiral of inner growth. Understand that your partner may be more developed in some areas of life than you and vice versa. Seek to meet each other at an equal level.

To summarize: pay attention to the context and dynamic of your relationship. If your connection is based on mutual love and respect then YES, it is possible to thrive and survive together. If you have a core need to connect with a spiritual partner, then NO, living with an "unspiritual" partner is unlikely to fulfill you. Although, before you jump to this conclusion, I ask you to reconsider what "spiritual" actually means to you – does it mean "spiritual" according to your path and beliefs, or something else? Also ask yourself, "Am I happy to do my thing and allow my partner to do theirs?" or do you both *absolutely* need to be on the same page?

Hopefully, you have a bit more clarity now as I know how complex and emotionally-charged this topic can be. Before you move onto the next section, it might be worth taking a break. What thoughts and feelings have arisen inside of you in response to this chapter? As always, I encourage you to write them down to explore more in-depth. This book hasn't just been created to read, but to *live*.

Relationship Demons

To end this chapter, we'll explore, with as much brevity and clarity as possible, some typical relationship demons that are *exclusive* to twin flame and soul mate relationships. Unfortunately, many of these demons run rampant, with an untold number of people in twin flame and soul mate communities confusing love with obsession, and growth with abuse. Here are the three major relationship demons to look out for:

Demon 1: Twin flame stalking (not chasing)

As we outlined earlier in this book, there are numerous stages of the twin flame union. The most difficult stage of the twin flame journey is the runner and chaser stage. In this stage, one partner simply cannot deal with the intensity of the connection (and the ensuing psychological and spiritual changes) and flees. The other, as a result, chases the runner and tries to preserve the love and connection desperately – hence why this is called the runner and chaser dynamic.

It is normal for a push-pull dynamic to occur in twin flame relationships. It is normal for the runner to want to run out of fear, and the chaser to want to chase out of loving commitment. Unfortunately, however, it is possible for the 'chaser' to become so obsessed with maintaining the relationship that the 'runner' is stalked, coerced, even manipulated into coming back. This situation is likely to happen in partners who have not done the inner work of exploring their issues with abandonment and loss of control.

As insanely painful as it is, the wisest thing to do in the runner and chaser stage is to let go and surrender. Although it is paradoxical, the more a person is chased, the farther away they will run. But once the chasing stops, the closer the runner will (often) move to re-establishing a connection again. We'll explore the topic of twin flame separation later in this book.

Demon 2: Justifying abusive behavior

Perhaps the most dangerous demon of all is confusing the challenges of twin flame relationships with blatant abuse. In fact, those who experience emotional or domestic violence may go so far as unconsciously *misusing* the twin flame label and applying it to their relationship as a way of soothing their suffering and giving it a purpose. I have seen this happen time and time again, and it's heartbreaking.

I want to be very clear here: a relationship that involves physical, emotional, psychological, or spiritual abuse *is not a twin flame relationship.* There is a difference between painful emotional and mental shifts in perception, and gaslighting. There is a difference between Life asking you to change and 'upgrade' as a result of your relationship, and your partner demanding that you change to appease their selfish, domineering desires. There is a difference between acting out wounds and perpetuating toxic narcissistic behavior. There is a difference between unconsciously triggering each other's shadows, and deliberately triggering the other with malice and hatred.

No matter what level of mental and emotional maturity both partners are at, *a twin flame relationship is based on mutual respect, compassion, and the desire to grow.* Any form of *intentionally inflicted* physical, emotional, psychological, or spiritual abuse should be seen as a BIG red flag – and I would advise running for the hills as soon as possible. If you suspect that you or a loved one is experiencing a situation of domestic or narcissistic abuse, I advise calling your local counseling hotline and seeking professional guidance immediately. A twin flame relationship, even though it can be painful and full of wearisome ego transformation, makes you feel empowered and free to be all that you're destined to be. If you don't feel this way, pay attention! Get help soon.

To help you determine whether your relationship may be abusive or not, please answer yes or no to the following statements:

- My partner gaslights me (causes me to question my own sanity)
- My partner punishes me with long silent treatments or physically assaults me

- My partner criticizes me and threatens that they'll leave/abandon me
- My partner uses spiritual terms to justify their bad behavior (e.g. "I'm an empath, that's why I cheated on you," "You're not as spiritually evolved as me, so you don't understand why I keep using this heroin," "Just let go of the past and raise your vibration, I won't hit you again")
- My partner intentionally violates my physical, emotional, mental or spiritual boundaries
- My partner uses me to feel good about themselves and then discards of me
- My partner never shows interest in what I love and value (they pretended to when we first got together)
- My partner declares that I'm their "twin flame" or "soul mate" but does it as a way of charming and manipulating me, as well as impressing others – but behind the scenes, I feel controlled and trapped

If you answered "yes" to any of the above statements, please take care of yourself. You are in an abusive relationship, and you need to call on outside support (e.g., a trusted friend, family member, therapist) to help you either navigate to the next steps or get out. No one has the right to abuse you, not even someone who calls themselves (or someone you think is) your "twin flame" or "soul mate."

Demon 3: Unnecessary pressure and expectations

Put simply, prematurely labeling your relationship as a 'twin flame' or 'soul mate' partnership can create unnecessary stress. "Why?" you may wonder. The answer is that when we label love too early, we create the unnecessary pressure of having to live up to these beliefs and expectations.

In the eloquent words of English poet David Whyte, "Naming love too early is a beautiful but harrowing human difficulty. Most of our heartbreak comes from attempting to name who or what we love and the way we love, too early in the vulnerable journey of discovery. We can never know in the beginning, in giving ourselves to a person, to a work, to a marriage or to a cause, exactly what kind of love we are involved with. When we demand a certain specific kind of reciprocation before the revelation has flowered completely we find ourselves disappointed and bereaved and in that grief may miss the particular form of love that is actually possible but that did not meet our initial and too specific expectations."

Relationships can suffer greatly when newly established when one or both partners immediately jumps to labeling the relationship as a 'twin flame' or 'soul mate' partnership. While this is understandable, and the ecstasy of newfound love can certainly make it seem so, be mindful and walk carefully. While categorizing your partnership as a twin flame or soul mate relationship doesn't always create harm, it can. I've heard of and seen many new relationships crumble under such pressure – particularly if one of the partners has underlying commitment issues stemming from the defense mechanisms they developed as an abandoned child.

The best thing to do, in my opinion, is to wait for a few months. See how the relationship develops. Give it some time to ripen. *Then* decide whether it is a twin flame, soul mate, or normal relationship. This way, you'll do your best to avoid falling into the trap of being with a 'false twin flame' or 'false soul mate,' and see the relationship for what it truly is.

Awake, Mindful, Present-Moment Love

As psychotherapist Neal M. Goldsmith writes, "In relationships, there are three broad stages (if we're lucky enough to get to the third phase): (1) infatuation, (2) the power struggle, and (3) a conscious relationship. During infatuation, the partner can do no wrong, whereas during the power struggle, each begins to wonder if they are going to get his or her needs met. Finally, after realizing that a vicious cycle has no end other than when you decide to make an ending, after realizing that the entire power struggle was a massive projection of one's own, one is finally ready to release one's childhood needs and focus on helping oneself and one's partner to feel awake, mindful, present-moment love."

It is normal to go through various stages in our soul mate and twin flame relationships. The second stage, the power struggle, comes in many shapes and forms as we've explored in this chapter. For some it may come in the form of conflicting beliefs, for others it may arise in runner and chaser dynamics, and still, for others, it may result in the breakdown and transformation of the ego. But be careful of abandoning your values, imposing your desires and expectations onto your partner, projecting your unresolved issues and needs onto them, and confusing love with abuse.

Yes, it is possible to get to the third stage of having a conscious relationship. But it won't be handed to you on a silver platter. You must work for it, like anything worthy of obtaining in life. We'll explore how to enter a conscious relationship later in this book, but first, let's explore what to do when your relationship falls apart. I know it may feel as though we're moving from bad to worse within this book! But we really must explore and understand everything that holds us back before we can enter a conscious relationship that brings us, our partners, and the world, love, joy, and spiritual expansion.

"I'm pretty sure I've met my true love but I don't understand what's wrong with me ... And I'm writing this email in the midst of my frustration, confusion, and fear. This is what's happening: I am dating an amazing guy, and I'm ready to be with him and never let go. We've known each other for many years but only recently started dating and talking more deeply. There are so many twin flame signs between us, we're like the yin and yang together, and there are even crazy synchronicities between our birth dates ... The problem is, I feel strange emotional turmoil. One moment I'm on a pink fluffy cloud, the next I feel like I never want to see him again! He's acting perfectly and there's no doubt I want to be with him, but one moment I'm ecstatic about the thought, the next moment I feel like throwing it all away and just LEAVING. What's wrong with me?"

– **JENNIFER** (sent via email)

CHAPTER 9

What to Do When Your Relationship Falls Apart

Someone can be madly in love with you and still not be ready. They can love you in a way you have never been loved and still not join you on the bridge. And whatever their reasons you must leave. Because you never ever have to inspire anyone to meet you on the bridge. You never ever have to convince someone to do the work to be ready. There is more extraordinary love, more love that you have never seen, out here in this wide and wild universe. And there is the love that will be ready.

— NAYYIRAH WAHEED

Losing your soul mate or twin flame is one of the hardest things you will ever experience. Whether through death, circumstance, or the inability to co-exist together, twin flame and soul mate separation is heart-wrenching. The pain you feel can be all-consuming, like a black vortex of quicksand. Your crushed hopes and dreams may cling to you like shrapnel as you walk through life feeling empty, numb, and lost. There is nothing in life that can quite compare to the grave and intense grief of losing your beloved.

In this chapter, we'll explore the painful topic of twin flame and soul mate separation. We'll also explore the runner and chaser stage that twin flames (and even soul mates) often go through, and how to make it through this distressing part of life's journey.

Causes of Separation

One of the most painful stages in the twin flame relationship is that of the "runner and chaser" dynamic. After the initial stages of ecstatic union and fairy-tale partnership, things start to heat up. Egos begin to clash, core wounds, insecurities, and traumas are rubbed raw, and shadow selves lash out. As a result, it's inevitable that almost every twin flame relationship will battle through drama and dysfunction at first. Understandably, this comes as a devastating shock. What happened to the perfect, rosy relationship paradise where everything was kisses and cuddles? At this point, many twin flame couples wind up confused and disorientated. Was it all a lie? Was it all an illusion?

The answer is *no*. The intensity you experienced was not a figment of your imagination. The sense of familiarity and déjà vu you felt wasn't a mystical apparition. It was real. Don't doubt it. It was simply buried under the layers of your damaged egos.

The sole purpose of twin flame relationships is to help us spiritually mature and become the best versions of ourselves possible. Perhaps the most powerful aspect of these connections is their ability to expose the dark, disowned, fractured parts of ourselves that we've hidden away (known as the 'shadow self') relentlessly. Furthermore, our twin flame relationships also have a great way of provoking our ego selves (that don't want to face the shadow self). Unfortunately, there comes a time in most twin flame relationships when enough is enough. The level of provocation and revelation can become so overwhelming to the ego that both partners in the twin flame relationship may become incapable of co-existing together. As a result, they separate. We'll help you to understand why exactly twin flames separate more below.

But first, you might be wondering whether the runner and chaser stage can occur in soul mate relationships. The answer is yes, it can – but often not to such a large degree. As the nature of soul mate relationships is more like water (as opposed to the fire that defines twin flame union), the issues faced are milder, but nevertheless still upsetting and destabilizing. If you identify yourself as being in a soul mate relationship, you will still greatly benefit from this chapter as soul mates can become twin flames, and vice versa.

Here are the biggest reasons why twin flames (and soul mates) can experience major relationship breakdown:

1. Psychological and spiritual immaturity

Life is a process of growth. Not only do our physical bodies grow, but our inner selves grow as well. One of the primary causes of twin flame separation is immaturity. When we're immature, we have low emotional intelligence meaning that we struggle to identify, manage and cope with our emotions and those of others. Not only that, but spiritual immaturity thrives in proportion to the stubbornness and magnitude of the ego. In other words, the bigger the ego self, the less harmony there is. The ego wants to believe itself to be charming, magnificent, all-knowing, and perfect. But when it is challenged in any way, shape, or form, there is hell to pay.

Almost all of us are ruled by the ego-self – if we weren't, we'd be enlightened. But not all egos are the same. There are strong egos, and there are weak egos. The stronger an ego is, the more likely it is to run away from a person or situation which makes it feel feeble. Twin flame relationships are one such place. In fact, twin flame relationships are essentially made to dissolve the ego – and the ego despises that.

2. Lack of self-love and respect

The main requirement needed to function smoothly in a twin flame relationship is self-love. Without learning how to love yourself first, there can be no genuine love for others. Instead, the love is tainted with neediness, co-dependency, and many unspoken "conditions." We can never give unconditional love to our partners without first showing fierce unconditional love towards ourselves. As a result of this, some twin flame relationships, unfortunately, crumble under the weight of insecurity and self-hatred.

3. More life lessons need to be learned

Life needs to prepare you before you enter a twin flame relationship. Sometimes this means that you need to enter other relationships, establish new friendships, or expand your life experience (travel, volunteer, get a new job) before you're ready. This is all a matter of trial and error. Some circumstances will bestow you with gentle insight, and others will leave you crushed and fighting for air. Whatever the case, don't shut yourself off from the world. The more you test your boundaries, the more you learn.

4. Healing needs to occur

Sometimes our twin flames show up at a point in life when we are suffering immensely. Our suffering may come from a tragedy, death, form of abuse or even another relationship breakup. We may not emotionally be in a place to open up yet. Therefore, a process of healing may be necessary first.

5. It's just not the time yet

Life can be mysterious. Sometimes twin flame separation occurs because the moment in time isn't right. Sometimes other journeys need to be completed, and other people need to be met. Sometimes we don't even know the reason why. The best thing to do in this situation is to surrender. This can be extremely hard, but trust that the experience will help you grow stronger and wiser.

When we separate from our flames, it's as though our entire lives have been shattered. The deep and intense love that we feel towards our twin flames makes any form of split agonizing and almost unbearable. But you *can* move through it. Have faith in yourself. You are stronger than you think. And although it may feel like everything is doomed, you never know what the future may bring. Below we'll explore how to recover from the twin flame separation.

How to Recover From Twin Flame Separation

Grief is an integral part of the healing process. My intention isn't to wave a magic wand and make your pain go away. Instead, my intention is to help expand your perspective and facilitate your recovery. You are a strong, worthy, spiritual being. You deserve to pick up the pieces of your heart, heal and move on with your life.

If you have experienced twin flame separation, I want you to know before you read the following list that although it felt as though your twin flame was your universe, you are capable of finding wholeness by yourself. Recovering from twin flame separation can take months, often years, and sometimes decades. But it's okay. Go at your own pace. Your healing process is unique, and as such, be gentle and patient with yourself. Here are some suggestions that may help ease the pain or prepare you for any grief that is to come:

1. Understand why the separation occurred

Often to find peace of mind, we need to understand why something in our lives occurred. If your separation was deliberate, you might like to explore the underlying reasons and causes. In understanding why you'll be able to learn valuable lessons about yourself that will help you to mature as a person.

2. Realize that twin flame separation makes you stronger

At first, this almost sounds like a sick joke. *Stronger?* How could that possibly be true? While losing your beloved temporarily causes immense sadness and distress, in the long term it can forge you into the person you were meant to become. Like a phoenix rising from the ashes, twin flame separation burns you so fiercely that you feel like useless, futile ash. But after a time, if you allow it to, this process of burning can give birth to strength, fortitude, and courage.

3. Allow yourself to mourn through self-expression

Intense emotions are scary. For this reason, most of us tend to hide, suppress or distract ourselves from feeling them. If you're experiencing extremely uncomfortable emotions such as depression, anger, and grief, slow down. Make space in your life to mourn. This isn't about self-pity, it's about actively experiencing your emotions. One of the best ways to actively experience emotions is through self-expression such as journaling, painting, playing an instrument, dancing, running, hiking, gardening, etc. Find what feels good, and go to that place. Don't remain static. Get moving. This is a powerful way to heal.

4. You are not your pain

When we are in an enormous amount of suffering it's easy for us to get stranded in victim roles. Melancholy is comfortable when it protects us from vulnerability. But remember this: pain is a passing sensation. It may be a very persistent emotion, but you are not your pain. You are so much more than your suffering. Making friends with pain, opening to it, and allowing it to teach you, shows you that pain is transient. Pain reveals to you the parts within yourself that haven't healed yet. Pain strips away the pretense and illusions and reveals to you the truth of what is there: your wounds, your insecurities, your beliefs, and your attachments. Pain shows you that you have loved deeply and fully. It reveals to you your own beauty, your own tender heart. Finally, when pain is fully accepted in the moment, it reveals a deeper truth: that you are limitless. You are not bound by any identity or story of pain. Pain is only a passing cloud on the sky that is You.

5. Our twin flames are not responsible for our happiness

Understand that twin flames powerfully facilitate our growth, but *they are not required for us to be happy.* Wholeness and fulfillment can be achieved without the presence of our twin flames. Unfortunately, a common myth about twin flames is that we somehow need them to be complete. This is false.

6. Integration

Integration is about taking your discoveries and actively applying them to your life. When you wholeheartedly surrender without resistance to what life is presenting to you, suffering ceases. Of course, this is easier done in theory than it actually is in real life. So be kind towards yourself. Go at your own pace. Integration takes time. And most importantly: be open to letting go of anything that no longer serves you.

Fierce Self-Love

Fiercely loving yourself – including all of your flaws, mistakes and shadow parts – is vital for healing. Often the main reason why we experience heartbreak in the first place is because of our own self-loathing and lack of self-understanding.

Be open to the reality that life is a mystery. You don't know what the future holds. You never know who may appear or re-appear in your life. Take comfort in this.

The Twin Flame Runner

This chapter wouldn't be complete without exploring the twin flame runner and chaser stage. Although not as severe as total relationship breakdown or loss, the runner and chaser stage can be extremely upsetting, confusing, alienating, and destabilizing.

Perhaps the hardest and most terrifying part of this relationship stage is that we simply don't know what the future of the relationship is. At least with total relationship loss there is a sense of finality, a sense of knowing where we are and what's happening. With the twin flame runner and chaser dynamic, we have no such certainty. Instead, there is a hellish void of confusion, fear, and desire that aches and claws inside of us.

What can be done? How can we get through such a painful stage? We'll explore that now. But first, let's examine the twin flame runner and chaser dynamic more closely.

What is the Twin Flame Runner and Chaser Dynamic?

When we think about the Twin Flame relationship in terms of stages, the Runner and Chaser dynamic represents stage six (please refer back to chapter three for a breakdown of the stages). It is preceded by a level of immense inner turmoil as personality differences, egos and old core wounds flare up. Eventually, as tensions rise to an explosive level, the only "way out" is to try and escape from the relationship in some shape or form. This process of distancing or "running" can be either physical or psychological, or both.

Often running away from the intense love within a twin flame relationship involves returning back to an ex-partner, traveling, silent treatments, constant arguments, workaholism or simply leaving for no apparent reason.

In my case, Luna was the chaser, and I was the runner – and these roles soon reversed in our relationship. When we first met the intensity of the connection was overwhelming for me. A door had suddenly opened out of nowhere, and the first urge I had was to run because I felt completely unprepared and vulnerable. Once I finally surrendered and decided I wanted to take a chance, Luna became the runner, and I switched roles to the chaser. As I helped to deprogram and untangle her from the cultish fundamentalist Christian beliefs she was immersed in, she would often become like a stone wall. At times she would hide in the bathroom or leave the house without a word and disappear for hours. No, we didn't physically separate (and that doesn't always happen in the runner and chaser stage), but emotionally and psychologically we were separated – and the wall between us sometimes felt impenetrable. For us, the runner and chaser dynamic lasted on and off for around three years. And the time varies for every twin flame couple; there is no right or wrong amount of time twin flames "should" be separated.

In the runner and chaser stage, the runner often represents the less advanced soul, and the chaser often represents the more spiritually advanced soul. In other words, while one partner is open to the purifying fires of love, the other finds the dissolution of their ego intimidating and too much to handle. This, of course, is not to say one partner is "better" or "superior" to the other. Remember that the roles can and do switch during the relationship.

Beware of Codependency

Here, it's vital to distinguish ego transformation (which involves the breakdown of barriers and blockages) with codependency in the runner and chaser stage. Many people, unfortunately, confuse codependency with twin flame love, and as a result, mistake the runner and chaser stage with codependent detachment. Codependency is the tendency to rely on our partners to fulfill all our emotional, mental, and spiritual needs. It's defined by unhealthy clinginess and is also referred to as "relationship addiction."

Before you read on, please ensure that you aren't in a codependent or unhealthy relationship. The difference between twin flame relationships and codependent relationships, is that twin flames relationships are defined by respect, equality, negotiation, and healthy boundaries. On the other hand, codependent relationships are characterized by feeling trapped, unequal, devalued and reliant on the other for a sense of self-worth. Unfortunately, it is possible to confuse codependency with twin flame love. Please be careful about confusing the two. If you think that you might have confused codependency with twin flame love, please see chapter ten (which explores the shadow side of love) within this book.

How to Move Through the Runner and Chaser Stage

If you love somebody, let them go, for if they return, they were always yours. If they don't, they never were.

– KAHLIL GIBRAN

If you are in the twin flame runner and chaser stage, you might be feeling extremely vulnerable, angry, overwhelmed or confused at the moment. This is understandable, and it's important to try and be gentle with yourself. You're going through a tough time, and it's okay (and essential) to practice some self-care and self-love.

Here are some suggestions and practices you might like to explore to make this stage easier (whether you're the runner or chaser):

1. Distinguish between intentional abuse and unintentional harm

Firstly, it's crucial to ensure that you're not actually in a codependent or emotionally abusive relationship. Unfortunately for some couples, this could be a genuine possibility. Don't confuse arguments, differences in character and insecurity for the more sinister forms of manipulation, control, and abuse. If you are in a twin flame relationship, it will be clear that your partner doesn't intend to cause you harm. The harm they cause you is unintentional and is a product of their own unresolved pain. However, if you're in an abusive relationship, it will be clear that the harm your partner causes you is intentional – by running away, they're trying to lure you into a toxic game of power and submission.

2. Think about what it is that triggers you in your partner's behavior

A trigger can be anything from a specific look, a tone of voice, a phrase, an action, or anything that "triggers" an emotional response within you. Once you have discovered what it is that triggers you (e.g., when your partner starts becoming opinionated), you may like to ask, "Why does that bother me so much?" Try to go deeper than answers like, "He thinks he knows everything," or "She isn't listening to what I'm saying." Find the emotion that is attached to the trigger – for instance, annoyance, bitterness or resentment – and keep digging deeper. It is likely that you will uncover many harmful ideals, beliefs, and personal issues beneath your layers of emotion.

Here is an example: You get offended and aloof every time your partner interrupts you. You then ask, "Why is that?" *You get upset because he isn't respecting what you're saying.* "Why is that a problem?" *That's a problem because it feels like he doesn't love you.* "Why is that an issue?" *You feel alone and abandoned.* Here we can see that the true issue is the underlying fear of being alone, abandoned, and unappreciated.

3. Learn to communicate with your twin flame openly

Open communication rarely comes naturally. Instead, it is something that the majority of us have to learn and master throughout our lives. When we fail to communicate openly, we hide our emotions, keep our thoughts and perspectives to ourselves, and don't speak up when something bothers us. If something bothers you about your partner's behavior, it is much better to openly and gently talk with them about it rather than hide it away and let it fester. Open communication is something the two of you should openly discuss and agree to work on. For an excellent open communication guide, I recommend reading *Nonviolent Communication: A Language of Life* by Marshall Rosenberg. This book has helped Luna and I tremendously.

4. Learn how to empathize with your twin flame's perspective

This can be extremely hard to do, especially when you're caught up in your own perceptions and feelings, but it is worth learning. Why? Developing this skill will help you to build empathy, and this will help your relationship to mature immensely. We recommend starting with the practice of mindfulness. Mindfulness can be practiced through traditional meditation practice, by learning to live in the moment, by spending time alone in reflection, by mindful breathing, and many other methods. The more proficient you become at learning how to observe instead of reacting to your emotions, the easier it will be for you to empathize with your twin flame. Remember that your partner grew up in a different context and therefore possesses different life experiences, different genetics, and a different personality from you. Remember that what they think, feel and believe is true for them but not necessarily true for you, and respect that.

5. Ask, "What am I being taught?"

Reflect on the fights you've had that may have led to the separation and ask yourself, "What was my twin flame trying to teach me through their words or actions?" Perhaps you need to develop more patience, understanding or forgiveness. In the end, our twin flames are like vessels through which the harshest, but most valuable lessons of life are transmitted. Only when you open yourself to learning these lessons can you grow as a person.

6. Forgive each other

Realize that both of you carry different types of pain. Every argument and every rash and hurtful decision is a product of unresolved pain. When you both learn to understand this, you can both forgive each other and allow the love you feel to cleanse all wounds.

7. Let go and let be

The more you pursue your twin flame, the more they will feel the urge to escape from you. It sounds paradoxical, but it's the painful reality. By trying to force or coerce your twin flame back into the relationship, you are unconsciously setting them against you and reinforcing their desire to escape from you. Remember, the reason why they've run away from you is that their ego cannot deal with the level of growth and transformation that is demanded of them.

Perhaps their ego never will be ready. You simply cannot know. This can be heartbreaking, but it's a truth that must be faced: you simply cannot know when (or if) your twin flame will ever be ready to be in a long-term relationship with you. However, by leaving them alone and giving them space, you will increase the chances that they'll want to rekindle a connection with you in the future. So let go and let be. Allow yourself to mourn. Refer back to the first part of this chapter on how to process and deal with grief. And try your very best to keep life moving with the understanding that the future is a mystery, and you never know what it holds. Even if the relationship doesn't actualize, you had the blessing of coming in contact with your twin flame – which is much more than many people have experienced. There is always the possibility of finding deep loving relationships in the future.

Not All Runners Are Worth Chasing

I often read and hear of people's struggles with the runner and chaser stage. Common stories run as follows:

- My twin flame just stopped contacting me and won't respond to any of my texts – this has been happening for months

- My twin flame's feelings have changed, and s/he has fallen out of love with me
- My twin flame cheated on me and left
- My twin flame left and is with a new partner now
- My twin flame refuses to talk to me after a fight we've had
- My twin flame is playing emotional games with me: s/he pulls me in then pushes me away

It's normal for there to be some level of physical, emotional, and/or psychological distancing (including going "no contact") during the twin flame relationship. It's also common for the "running" to be more subtle and enacted in the form of petty fights, excuses, dramas, and self-created obstacles which prevent authentic twin flame union. But there comes a time when we have to be realistic and face the hard truth.

If your twin flame has acted out against you or is playing games with you, it's worth asking the following questions:

(1) Is your "twin flame" actually a false twin flame?

(2) Is it *worth* chasing the "runner"?

Remember, not all runners are worth chasing. Not all flames are ready to be in a serious relationship that is committed to spiritual growth and transformation. By pursuing them and refusing to let them go, we can easily make ourselves sick with longing and heartbreak. The best thing to do in this situation – while extremely painful – is to let them go. We cannot force them to awaken. We cannot *make* them mature or convince them to commit. That decision must come from deep within *them*.

Often the case is that the *more* we push them, the *more* they push away. This push-pull dynamic can be crazy-making and can carry on for months or even years. For the sake of your own sanity and emotional wellbeing, the best thing to do is to let go and let Life take over. This is a lesson in surrender, and at this time, it's crucial that you understand the fact that your twin flame doesn't complete you or make you whole. Your soul is already whole, and with or without your twin flame, you still have an amazing journey full of purpose, growth, and metamorphosis ahead of you.

On the other hand, sometimes the people who we think are our "twin flames" are actually our soul teachers (please refer to chapter two for a more in-depth look at soul teachers). Soul teachers are here to intentionally or unintentionally teach us lessons to help us grow. Mistaking them for our twin flames is easy. Please revisit chapter three if you'd like to learn how to spot a false twin flame.

Surrender

Perhaps this is why it's so very difficult to lose a soulmate. You don't just lose your companion. You don't just lose your friend. You don't just lose your lover. You lose your portal to divinity. You lose your gateway to God. You lose the whole bloody universe. And then you find it again. In your heartbreak. In your healing. In the learning of the lessons that expand you.

– JEFF BROWN

Perhaps the key takeaway from this chapter is the importance of surrendering. Surrender means letting go and allowing Life to take over. Surrender means relinquishing the desire to coerce, control, and escape. In essence, surrender is a quality that both the runner and chaser within the twin flame relationship must learn in order to progress to the next higher levels of union. Even if the relationship wasn't meant to be (as is sometimes the case with twin flame and soul mate partnerships), vital lessons were learned that enriched the soul and helped it to expand. What a great blessing.

I leave you with a heartfelt wish:

May your heart, mind, and soul surrender to whatever Life presents you with. May you love and forgive yourself. May you love and forgive your partner. May your heart heal and open. May you be at peace.

In the next chapter, we'll explore the most essential – but most ignored – aspect of creating a strong, mature, and awakened relationship: the shadow side of love. Only by bravely facing the dark side can we emerge as beacons of unified light within this world.

"As the years progressed, I kept desperately trying to get him to be a part of my life. I think this is what they call the "dark night of the soul." I went through many bouts of messaging and texting him, even going as far as sending him ten page letters about my feelings, but also my madness. It forced him to move deeper and deeper away. He'd either ignore me or get mad at me saying that he "doesn't remember who I am." It was an extremely tough time and so unlike me to be toxically attached to him. Just when he'd given me another chance, I'd ruin it with crazy desperation and clinginess."

– MEGAN (sent via letter)

CHAPTER 10

The Shadow Side of Seeking Love

Most people want love. The craving for approval and affection from others is embedded into our DNA. There's probably nothing else on earth (other than the survival instinct) that is as strong and primal as the longing for love.

We need to belong. We *need* to feel loved. This is all normal. It's a wonderfully exciting and ecstatic quest that we all walk sooner or later. But what happens when our search for love becomes tainted with unconscious motives? What happens when our search for love comes from a place of avoidance and fear?

The answer is that we suffer. But we don't just experience garden-variety-type-suffering, we go through *cyclical suffering*, meaning that we repeat the same toxic patterns over and over again. In other words, when the love we have obtained doesn't distract us from ourselves enough, we jump ship. We break up. We divorce. We try to find someone new who will fill that hole inside of us. We get bored or scared. We leave. Then the cycle starts again. This is the shadow side of twin flame and soul mate relationships. And it can and will happen if we aren't mindful.

In this chapter, we'll examine the dark side of seeking twin flame and soul mate relationships. While it may feel uncomfortable and at times even upsetting to examine our shadows, we need to be honest with ourselves. If we are to enter healthy, strong, stable, and spiritually nourishing partnerships, we need to come from a space of truth, self-understanding, compassion, and clarity. It's only when these darker areas go ignored or unexplored that the shadows hiding within us rear their ugly heads and wreak havoc.

One of the biggest shadows that most people experience is using love as a form of escapism. We'll examine that first. Later, we'll explore other common romantic shadows that emerge on our paths.

Why We Use the Search For Love to Escape Ourselves

As children, most of us were conditioned to believe that romantic love was the greatest pursuit in life. In a sense, we were *programmed* to believe that romantic love would solve all our problems – it's part of our internal hardware, and that is why it's so deeply ingrained and pervasive.

From the tender age of two or three, we were read fairy tales that depicted princess and princesses falling in love and eventually getting married. How many times do you remember hearing the sentence, "...and they lived happily ever after"? These whimsical beliefs surrounding romantic love were deeply ingrained in our fragile young minds.

As we grew up, the idea that the search for love is the almighty Purpose of Life was reinforced by Hollywood films, books, magazines, pop songs, and even self-improvement workshops – and every day it continues to be bolstered by social media, Hollywood, and the people around us. Can you see why so many of us fall into the trap of using love as a form of escapism? We were virtually brainwashed as children to see it as the only path to happiness and fulfilment.

Not only were we brainwashed as children to see the pursuit of love as the meaning of life, but as we grow older, it becomes a drug that numbs us and helps us to avoid our pain. Those who have experienced the high of falling in love will understand that the feeling is *incomparable* to anything else in life: it is pure ecstasy – and much better and long lasting than the drug variety. Life suddenly feels magical and awe-inspiring again. Anything feels possible. Tidal waves of joy wash over you and you feel warm, tingly, elevated, and drunk all at once. Optimism replaces your negative outlook on life, and you feel like a new person!

Falling in love is an amazingly transcendental adventure. It is a great blessing to experience something so pure and sacred. So how can such an experience become corrupted? The answer is that our motivations sully the experience – but these motivations are usually entirely unconscious (that is, below our conscious awareness).

When finding love is used as a way of escaping ourselves, *it becomes more like a drug to numb our pain, rather than a spiritual journey.* The experience is cheapened as conditions are placed upon the relationship for it to work. The dominant unspoken condition is: "You must make me happy and distract me enough from my pain and emptiness for this to work." When this condition isn't met consistently, the relationship begins to sour, decompose, and break apart.

As humans, we are quite resourceful when it comes to escaping our inner sorrow, rage, loneliness, and emptiness. Virtually anything – so long as it keeps us distracted – can be used to bypass facing and overcoming this suffering. Popular examples include food, TV, gossip, drama, sex, partying, workaholism, social entanglements, and of course, drugs and alcohol. But perhaps most dazzling of all is the pursuit of love.

What better way to distract yourself and fill the void inside of you than chasing after your soul mate or twin flame? It is a quest that promises to give you a "happily ever after" (and therefore solve all of your problems) – not to mention it's so damn exciting and a million times better than a telenovela. Oh, and there's no stigma attached to using love as your form of escapism, unlike drugs. So you get the social approval as well. How convenient.

10 Signs You're Using Love to Escape Yourself

Love is a touchy topic, and many people prefer to live in a fantasy land rather than in reality – which I understand. But love doesn't need to be used as a form of escapism for it to be intoxicating and profoundly life-changing. In fact, if you are genuinely wanting to experience authentic and mature love, I recommend asking yourself the following question: "Am I using the search for love to escape myself?" If you dare to answer the question, be proud of yourself for taking this courageous step. Honesty is the best policy when it comes to love (and basically everything in life).

Signs that you're using the search for love to escape yourself include the following:

1. You believe that you're "not complete" without a romantic partner/soul mate/twin flame
2. You can't cope with being alone or spending time by yourself
3. You are a Relationship Hopper: you jump from one relationship to another quickly
4. Your life centers around the pursuit of finding your One True Love
5. All of your personal hopes and dreams are wound up in your search for love
6. On some level, you believe that the Perfect Relationship will solve all of your problems
7. You have had dramatic and stormy relationships in the past
8. You feel a looming/subtle sense of anxiety and endangerment in your relationships

9. You want a deep and soulful relationship, but you always somehow end up with shallow/incompatible partners
10. You consider yourself a Romantic or an Idealist (or both)

Why did I choose these signs? If you're using the search for love as a form of escape, you will be driven by romantic idealism and the belief that your One True Love will complete you. This is a fallacy because it makes your self-esteem, self-worth, and happiness dependent on another person, making you feel a sense of constant underlying anxiety and endangerment.

Once you do find a partner, you will attract a person who fulfills your unconscious need to escape and numb yourself. But because your relationship is based on this unconscious desire to numb and escape, once it stops fulfilling this function, it quickly begins to disintegrate, leaving you heartbroken. Because you feel empty or alone inside, you can't stand being by yourself so you will hop onto another relationship, and another, and another, leaving you exhausted.

Sound like a familiar pattern?

How to Experience Authentic Love (Without the Addiction & Escapism)

When your search for soul mate or twin flame love is driven by the unconscious motives of escaping or numbing your inner pain/emptiness, you will always be unhappy. After a while, you might even give up hope of *ever* having a satisfying relationship. Worst of all, you might become a cynic and declare that romantic love is pointless or not for you.

In order to carefully remove yourself from this sticky web of suffering, you have to, first and foremost, be self-aware. You must clearly and honestly OWN this as your issue that must be worked through. There can be no growth or progression without this first step. A similar rule applies for addicts: in order to heal, they must first get over the denial stage and agree that there is a serious issue.

Love, in a way, can become an addiction. Yes, it is a socially approved addiction, but it is an addiction nonetheless. And we all know what addiction does to your life: it can quickly turn it into a living hell.

If you think you might be struggling with love escapism, here are some steps you can take to experience a deep, authentic, and genuinely magical relationship:

1. Stop chasing love

Understand that chasing love only creates more frustration and hopelessness. Really try to understand this concept and dig your teeth into it. Chasing happiness creates suffering. The more you chase it, the more it evades you because happiness only ever exists in the present moment. It's perfectly normal to want to find your twin flame or soul mate, but be careful of dedicating *all* of your time to that pursuit.

2. Replace your chasing with a healthier form of escapism

It is very difficult just to stop doing something you're habitually inclined to do, cold turkey. In order to temporarily prevent yourself from relapsing into old habits, find something else to distract yourself with or pursue.

Healthy forms of escapism may include learning a new skill, creating goals, and pursuing new hobbies such art, craft, cooking, reading, blogging, vlogging, dressmaking, animal rearing, gardening, yoga, tai chi, martial arts, traveling, veganism, horse riding – you name it. Find something you're interested in or passionate about and channel your energy towards learning about and mastering it. (On a side note, to help you set new habits, I strongly recommend reading *The Power of Habit* by Charles Duhigg.)

3. Creatively explore what you're trying to avoid

Spend time thinking about what feeling or state of being you're trying to avoid. Go as deep as you can and keep asking "what is behind this feeling?" For example, you might think you're trying to avoid boredom, but if you go even deeper, you might find that what you're actually afraid of is loneliness. Or you might think that you're afraid of being lonely, but what you're really afraid of is emptiness and disconnection from your soul. Common things people run away from include self-loathing and poor self-esteem, heartbreak, grief, depression, fear, anger, loneliness, and emptiness. Creatively expressing these thoughts and emotions will not only serve as a form of emotional catharsis but also as a way of experiencing more clarity. I recommend journaling and art therapy as a way of diving into your inner landscape.

4. Face and embrace your demons

Facing and embracing your demons (i.e., Shadow Work) is about coming in contact with that darker and hidden side of yourself which you would normally prefer to avoid altogether. Once you have discovered what your greatest fear is, there are only two paths. The first path is to avoid facing your fear (and continue suffering) willfully. The second path is to face your fear (and eventually experience freedom) courageously. Mind you, Shadow Work is not for the faint of heart. You must seriously commit to this work, but it's okay to take breaks. One simple place to start with Shadow Work is by paying attention to your dreams. What repetitive elements or storylines keep emerging, and what do you think they mean? Keep a record in a dream diary.

5. Let love come to you

Instead of chasing love, let it come to you when the time is right. The Universe can't be forced or manipulated into giving you what you want. Be humble and let go of the need for control. Your soul mate/twin flame will come when the time is right, and not a moment sooner. But although you can't control when your beloved appears in your life, you *can* control how receptive and open you will be to such a meeting.

6. Love and respect yourself

Would you like to meet your soul mate/twin flame and have a happy and fulfilling relationship? The best way to be open to this experience is by learning how to love and respect yourself. When your love quest is motivated by unconscious fear or self-loathing, your relationship will inevitably be tainted. But when you already feel confident and secure within yourself, then your relationship is more likely to be rich and rewarding. Why? The answer is that you are not relying on your partner for validation or self-worth: you already possess these qualities. So learn how to be whole and complete by yourself, and your joy will be doubled when you meet your beloved – not out of quiet desperation – but out of the sheer delight of sharing your life with another. (Please see the next chapter for some self-love practices.)

7. Learn to enjoy being alone

Break free from the societal conditioning which makes you believe that your self-worth, fulfillment, and fundamental wholeness is based on whether you're in a relationship or not. Learn to love being alone. Enjoy your own company. Explore who you are. Do some soul-searching. You don't need another person to fulfill you. As a person who has found their twin flame and is in a wonderfully strong relationship, I can tell you that your partner will not fulfill you. Only you can fulfill you. *Your soul is already complete.* You just need to break through the obstacles of the ego to realize that. Romantic partners can be our companions, confidants, best friends, lovers, spiritual catalysts, and so much more, but they do not complete us. I know that we have repeated this philosophy ad nauseam, but such a mentality (of wanting another to complete you) only creates profound unhappiness and confusion. It must be replaced!

You Are Already Whole

It can take years, sometimes decades or even lifetimes to discover one of the most simple truths of all: you are already whole.

Most of us have heard quotes and speeches from mystics, spiritual teachers, and enlightened folk talk about this. Yet most of us don't truly take it to heart. *True happiness and wholeness originate from within you.*

Anything outside of you that is a source of happiness will eventually perish or be taken away. All false ideals, beliefs, and thought patterns will eventually be revealed and destroyed.

When everything outside of you is taken away, what remains? When your health, good looks, riches, family, friends, and yes, even soul mates and twin flame are taken away, what remains?

Most of us are too scared to answer this question. We are terrified to face our inner emptiness and loneliness face-on. We feel unable to face our soul loss: the profound loss of contact we have with our souls.

But the moment we are ready to face this inner emptiness is the moment we can dive into it through shadow work. The more inwards we travel, the more we discover something amazing: the presence of our soul begins to emerge. The more blockages in the form of unresolved pain and conditioned beliefs we remove, the brighter our souls become.

As we begin to connect with our essence, our wholeness, our very souls, we start letting go of all the beliefs that obscured our inner Light. We refer to this as inner work or doing the work of the soul.

The notion that you are already Whole may seem hilarious, even an insult considering all the pain you might be struggling with. But the only way for you to find out whether this statement is real or not is to go exploring for yourself: to do the inner work. Only then can you discover that everything you've been suffering is a result of the thoughts, ideas, and beliefs you've innocently subscribed to. And your soul mate or twin flame can't do that work for you. Only you can.

Romantic Love is a Divine Catalyst

The deepest desire of our heart is to give love and to feel love. I want you to know that there's nothing wrong with pursuing the love of your soul mate or twin flame. There is absolutely nothing wrong with craving for and seeking out someone to love. This is a normal feeling.

But don't base your happiness around it.

When you start believing that someone "out there" will complete you and give you everything you've ever been searching for … you immediately unlock the door of suffering. You quickly unleash the hellhounds of grief, anger, loneliness, and fear. Please avoid that suffering if you can.

While our soul mates and twin flames do not complete us, they do act as divine catalysts. What do I mean by divine catalysts? I mean that our soul mates and twin flames help us to grow in ways we never dreamed of on an emotional, psychological, and spiritual level. And while these relationships do not complete us, they *do* help us access the fulfillment that is already buried away deep inside of us.

I will repeat this again: soul mate and twin flame relationships help us to access the wholeness that is already within us, but they do not, in and of themselves, complete us. *How can anything outside of you that can be taken away, complete you?* Think about that for a while.

Your Heart Wants to Give and Feel Love

The deepest need of every human being is to give and feel love. Romantic love is one of the closest experiences to our true nature, which is why we obsess about it so much.

When we fall in love, our hearts are open, and a sense of freedom fills us. This experience is very similar to what we call liberation, moksha, Oneness or enlightenment. But the key thing to remember here is that romantic love is not the same as unconditional love.

What we are searching for, when all has been said and done, is unconditional love. And relying on another person to give you that will always bring you great grief and suffering. So if you would like to avoid this suffering and experience the everlasting love within your soul, you can practice these bits of advice:

1. Realize that your heart wants to give and feel love
2. Understand and discover for yourself that romantic love cannot complete you
3. See that romantic love helps you to deepen your spiritual growth, but it will not give you everything you've ever dreamed of
4. When you are ready, face your inner emptiness – what are you running away from?
5. Learn to stop chasing after happiness in the form of other people or ideals
6. Explore inner work (self-love, inner child work, shadow work) as a map that can help you with your inner journey

I hope these suggestions help. Remember, even when you do find the love of your life, emptiness, and darkness will eventually return. This feeling of incompletion might arise after one, two, five or ten years, but it will always return.

As P. T. Mistlberger writes in his book *Rude Awakening*, "The notion of a perfect 'soul mate' and the idea of the ultimate romance, as well as the anguished longing to find one's perfect match, is ultimately based on romanticizing the pain of incompletion. The underlying sense – the core-level pain – of feeling incomplete is always fundamentally spiritual, meaning it is originating in the contraction and 'closed fist' of fear and mistrust, and the profound sense of alienation and separation we experience from both life, ourselves, and our highest potential. With the introduction of the notion of ideal romantic love – the perfect soul mate – the pain of separation from our highest potential gets redirected into the pain of separation from our true soul mate. In other words, the idea of our highest potential gets reduced to an idealized, imagined other person, and moreover, a person who we imagine to be our potential ideal partner."

By choosing to take off the rose-tinted glasses and face reality, you will be taking a courageous step towards the truth that *no one* needs to, or ever can, complete you. Your soul is already Whole.

Other Common Relationship Shadows

A lot can be said about the dark side of twin flame and soul mate relationships. But at risk of overwhelming you, I'll keep it simple and succinct. Also, as these shadows can feel intimidating, uncomfortable, and dense to read through, I encourage you to go at your own pace – or skip this part until you feel ready. You can always move to the next chapter if you're not ready to dive deep.

With that being said, here are eight shadows to be mindful of:

1. Projection

Projection is a mental defense mechanism we (unconsciously) use to avoid certain negative truths about ourselves by displacing them onto others instead. Projection can also involve seeing in another person something *good* that is actually within ourselves. Whether good or bad, projection is generally detrimental to our wellbeing. When we cannot claim our positive and negative qualities as *ours*, we burden our partners with them and struggle to perceive reality clearly. Of course, it is sometimes possible to project a trait of ours onto our partner that they *actually do* possess (this is called 'projecting onto reality'). But usually, projection involves misperceiving our partners and thus harming them and ourselves. For instance, we might feel paranoid that they're not telling us the truth when in reality we are projecting *our own* dishonesty and lack of transparency onto them. Another example is projecting our own disowned confidence and assertiveness onto our partner and admiring them for a quality that we feel we lack (but actually do have).

2. Idealization

When we idealize our soul mate or twin flame we only see the version of them that *we* want to see – and usually this version is highly romanticized to the point of near perfection. Those who idealize their partners once again refuse to face reality and suffer tremendously when their rose-tinted glasses are shattered. In fact, when one partner in a relationship is idealizing the other, the idealized partner will often act out unconsciously in an attempt to break the illusion. Examples of acting out may include arguing, betraying trust, and behaving self-destructively. It's essential that we realize that our soul mates and twin flames are *human* and have flaws like any other person.

3. Erotomania

This shadow can actually occur when we're single and pursuing our twin flame or soul mate. Due to an intense desire to unite with our spiritual partner, we might develop the delusional belief that another person (whom we are fixating on) is in love with us, despite the clear evidence against it. We might obsess over the person and try to analyze any little sign of interest that they show toward us. Sometimes, erotomania verges into dangerous territory, particularly when the one we're fixating on is a narcissist who enjoys the lavish attention and toying with our emotions mercilessly.

4. Denial

Denial is a mental and emotional defense mechanism that helps to protect us from truths that are too hard for us to bear. In the realm of twin flame and soul mate relationships, denial is often paired with other shadows such as projection and idealization and supports them by attempting to preserve our rose-tinted illusions. Denial can also serve to keep us locked within false twin flame and soul mate relationships. For example, we may have hung our hopes and dreams on a particular person so intensely that any red flags that emerge within the relationship are explained away or ignored – this is denial. When we refuse to acknowledge reality, when we avoid facing the clear existence of something, we are in denial.

5. Repression

To achieve the picture-perfect (idealized) relationship we envision, we may sometimes unconsciously repress any feelings of emptiness, unhappiness, or anger we feel. Repression means pushing something out of awareness and locking it up within the unconscious mind. Usually, it's easy to tell whether we have repressed something by observing how intense and dramatic our dreams are. Repression is a normal shadow that most people experience at some point because it flies directly in the face of what we've been taught about love (i.e., that it will solve all our problems). But burying our unresolved issues and wounds won't make them go away – nor will it make our relationships the dreamy paradises we've fantasized about.

6. Introjection

Introjection is the opposite of projection: instead of seeing in another what we possess, we 'absorb' certain traits from our partners that aren't actually ours. Introjection occurs when one or both people in a relationship have weak or tenuous identities. When the sense of self is not strong, it's easy to become a sponge and take on the positive and negative traits of our partners, often without knowing.

While this is not always a bad thing (in the case of qualities such as generosity and curiosity), it can become detrimental, particularly when we are acting out patterns of behavior that are self-destructive (like paranoia, compulsive addictions, etc.). If you 'don't feel like yourself' or have adopted certain qualities that you never possessed before your relationship, you might be experiencing introjection. Try to be mindful of what you want to welcome into your daily life, and what doesn't serve you. Understanding and exploring who you truly are will help prevent against introjection.

7. Codependency

Codependency is the tendency to excessively rely on our relationships for our emotional and psychological fulfillment. When we boil it down, codependency is essentially relationship addiction. Although it may be uncomfortable to face, codependency is a *major* issue when it comes to seeking out and attempting to thrive within spiritual partnerships. When we feel as though we are "nothing" without our relationships and when we uncomfortably cling to our partners, we are struggling with codependency. In codependent relationships, the issue is usually two-sided meaning that it's not just your fault – it may also be reinforced by your twin flame or soul mate who may play the 'giver-rescuer' or 'taker-victim' role. In other words, if you're in a codependent relationship, you will both be enabling each other in some way. The cure for codependency starts with self-love and the willingness to find a sense of security and worthiness inside oneself, rather than in the relationship.

8. Enmeshment

Enmeshment occurs in soul mate and twin flame relationships when both partners have a weak sense of self. Similar, to codependency, there is an unhealthy reliance on the other partner to provide a sense of worthiness and sense of self. But the difference, when it comes to enmeshment, is that each partner is not permitted to play a unique and dynamic role (i.e., be their authentic selves). Instead, there is a specific 'script' that must be adhered to at all times and certain roles that must be preserved and played out no matter what. In the case of soul mate and twin flame relationships, it's very possible to play out the exclusive role of "soul mates" and "twin flames" who are perfectly and wonderfully happy all the time. Can you feel how fake and limiting that would be? Just playing one role – and not being permitted to play others – is suffocating and opposed to spiritual growth. Certainly, it's useful to have these labels, but it's important to integrate them and not use them as a cage to trap ourselves in.

These eight shadows (or "karmic patterns") can occur in all types of soul mate and twin flame relationships at any stage of the journey. If you had an emotional or visceral reaction to any of the above shadows, write it down and explore it. Any reaction you have will be a sign that you've stumbled across a dark area that needs to be explored either alone, with your partner, or with a relationship counselor. The solution to each one of these shadows is inner work (self-love, inner child work, shadow work). Remember that no true change can occur without going to the root cause within ourselves. We'll explore the three inner work practices more in-depth in the next chapter. But for now, take some time to reflect on any shadows that have called to you. How do you feel? What memories arise? Do you feel defensive, angry, or any other strong emotions? Remember, it's okay to feel anything and everything that arises within you. You are not alone. All relationships have shadows, but they are pathways toward illumination and spiritual transformation.

In the final chapter of this book, we'll explore the *ultimate purpose* of twin flame and soul mate relationships: to serve as spiritual catalysts for personal, relational, and global transformation. Without a unified vision and purpose, twin flame and soul mate relationships can feel lackluster and directionless. So let's get started …

Love does not consist in gazing at each other, but in looking outward together in the same direction.

– Antoine de Saint-Exupery

CHAPTER 11

How to Use Your Relationship as a Spiritual Catalyst

By now, after having read through the meat and bones of this book, you might be wondering what's next. What happens once we find our soul mate or twin flame, have moved through the first intoxicating (but hectic) phase of ecstatic union, and are in a stable relationship?

The answer is simple. *The ultimate purpose of the soul mate and twin flame relationship is to serve as a spiritual catalyst.* These relationships exist to help you, your partner, and the world at large grow and transform. Yes, there is a higher purpose beyond the magic and romance, and that purpose involves influencing the planet (and the billions of people that live in it) at large.

The electric nature of soul mate and twin flame relationships is such that major change (when done intentionally) is inevitable. When I write "electric," what I really mean is that a tremendous torrent of energy exists between two people in a spiritual partnership. The more both partners seek conscious growth, the more layers of shadow are removed, and the more light shines through. When two beacons of light combine it is the equivalent of a solitary lighthouse turning into a searing laser beam. Can you see how powerful this fusion of energy could be?

But to create a mature, awakened, and dynamic relationship that creates major changes within ourselves and the world, we need to commit to the inner work. This is by no means an easy path, but it is a profoundly worthy one full of rich and bountiful rewards.

As transpersonal therapist P.T. Mistlberger reminds us, "Probably the most difficult of all forms of inner work is so-called relationship work, or 'interpersonal processing' … The whole function of relationship of any sort is to confront, slowly and steadily, our personal blocks to remembering, seeing, and realizing our higher nature and best possibilities."

There are three ways our soul mate or twin flame relationships can catalyze profound change. The first is self-transformation, the second is other-transformation, and the third is world transformation. We'll explore these three levels, and how to accomplish them within your relationship in this chapter.

Spiritual Partnerships and Self-Transformation

In order to attract and maintain romantic and spiritual partnerships, you must be what it is that you're seeking. That is, you always need to put forth what you want to attract.

– WAYNE DYER

The purpose of our relationships is to help us learn and grow. However, not only do soul mate and twin flame relationships help us to accomplish this, but they also help us to awaken spiritually. And as we've learned earlier in this book, spiritual awakening is a deep process of transformation where the presence of our soul manifests, and our True Nature becomes apparent.

But the question must be asked, how can we grow and awaken in a relationship when we're overtaken with wounds, traumas, unhealthy defense mechanisms, and psychological complexes? The answer is that growth is nearly impossible when there is an inner goblin within us viciously undermining all our sincere efforts. How can we transform when there is an intense unconscious drive towards self-sabotage and self-destruction? No matter how pure, noble, and earnest our efforts, they will be ruthlessly thwarted by this goblin that lurks within us.

Thankfully, there is a way of facing these shadows and preventing them from controlling our lives. The solution is a process called inner work. Below, we'll explore each of the three paths that compose inner work.

Path 1 – Self-Love

We have previously explored inner work in this book and seen that there are three levels: self-love, inner child work, and shadow work. The reason why there are three levels is to prevent us from going too deep too quickly (which may be overwhelming, traumatizing, and totally counterproductive).

For instance, if you were to start with shadow work instead of practicing self-love first, you would most likely become crippled with self-hatred and anxiety. Building strong and healthy self-esteem is vital before moving on to inner child work and shadow work. Think of self-love as the foundation of your inner work practice that you can always return to, no matter how uncomfortable or challenging your inner work appears to be.

To practice inner work in the context of your twin flame or soul mate relationship, it is, therefore, best to start with self-love. Below, you'll find some simple self-love ideas to practice in the container of your relationship:

1. Relax together

Plan a relax-and-unwind afternoon or evening with your partner each week. You might decide to get a massage together, go watch the sunset, take a walk in nature, or anything that calms the two of you. This is also a great way to spend quality time together and strengthen your spiritual bond.

2. Eat healthy food

Commit yourself to healthy eating. The food you eat impacts your body, mind, emotions, and spiritual connection. Make a habit of cooking together (if possible) or finding clean recipes to enjoy. Improving the quality of your food is a form of self-love and self-care.

3. Exercise together

Go for a morning or afternoon walk with each other. If you prefer, jog instead, or attend a gym. Taking care of your body is one of the simplest self-loving things you can do.

4. Pull a card

In the morning, make a habit out of pulling one card with your partner from an oracle or tarot deck. Discuss the card you each pulled and how its message applies to your self-love journey.

5. Ask for feedback

Ask your partner to point out areas in your daily life or spiritual journey where more self-love is needed. Be mindful during this exercise as you might feel defensive or embarrassed. These are normal feelings to have, but try to breathe through them and remain open. Remember, your partner is trying to help you at *your* request. So strive to be receptive and thankful for any information you receive.

6. Compliment and express gratitude

Regularly say "thank you," "I understand," "you're beautiful," "you're handsome," "you're wonderful," "I love you," and so forth to your partner. Compliment them and feel sincere gratitude for their existence in your life. Your partner is a mirror of you, so the more kind you are to them, the more they'll reflect that love right back at you! This is a beautiful self-love activity.

One thing you might like to do for your partner to show them how much you value them is to create a gratitude jar. I created one of these for Luna a few years ago entitled "101 Things I Love About Lunita" and gave it to her on our anniversary. When you create something with your hands and give it from your heart, not only do you make yourself feel wonderful but also your partner at the same time.

7. Practice open communication

Openly communicate what you're feeling, and ask your partner to do the same. Without open and clear communication, relationships suffer tremendously. Remember, your partner may know the heights and depths of you, but they can't always read your mind. Please don't expect them to immediately understand what's going on within you as this can place unnecessary pressure on them. In fact, those who carry the belief that their partners should be able to read them all the time are regressing back to pre-infancy. After all, a baby's needs were all met in the womb. But now we're in the big wide world. This is adulthood. Our partners aren't our parents, and we shouldn't expect them to read us properly unfailingly. Although it may feel uncomfortable, simply and plainly explaining what's going on will help your partner to help you.

All of the above activities can be practiced alongside your soul mate or twin flame. Remember to take it slowly. Pressuring your partner (whether directly or indirectly) to do these self-love activities with you is not very self-loving! In fact, by coercing your partner, you might just do the opposite: harm both them and yourself. Please communicate with each other and mutually agree to try an activity. If there is motivation on both sides, you'll have much more long-term success with these practices.

Once both of you have developed stable and positive self-esteem and have practiced self-love together, it's time to move on to inner child work.

Path 2 – Inner Child Work

Inner child work can be tricky as it starts to enter the world of wounds, traumas, and triggers. The most vital thing to remember when it comes to this level of inner work is to do everything *gently and slowly*.

To be successful at inner child work (but keep in mind that this work is a lifelong process), you'll both need to be capable of holding space for each other. To hold space means to be completely present with the other person. In other words, holding space means allowing the other to be completely heard, seen, and understood. I'm not talking about trying to fix, give advice to, or pathologize the other person here. When I say "holding space," I mean it in the most simple way possible: just being 100% there for the person, without trying to change or force advice onto them.

Ways to learn how to hold space for your partner can include practicing present-moment mindfulness, mastering the art of active listening, and emptying your mind of judgments (through a practice such as meditation). It's also important to know your limits, particularly if you're already feeling stressed and overwhelmed. You can always mutually agree to postpone the inner child work to a later date and practice self-care in the meantime. This must be done with the utmost delicacy, consideration, and emotional perceptivity. Once you have practiced holding space for each other (for lighter, more everyday topics), you can move on to heavier and more emotionally-charged topics – like both of your childhood memories, fears, and wounds.

Below, you'll find some inner child work ideas to explore within your soul mate or twin flame relationship. Remember, inner child work has the potential to initiate a tremendous level of spiritual transformation within both you and your partner – so be prepared! And again, be gentle and go slowly:

1. Ask for a hug

When you feel sad, afraid or any other intense emotion in daily life, ask for a hug from your partner. Not only will this help support your inner child, but it will help you to feel contained. Have a conversation with your partner and encourage them to reach out for emotional support as well when they feel overburdened. A hug is a simple wordless expression of love, but it speaks volumes to the smaller vulnerable part of you.

2. Have fun and play together

Introduce play into your life together. Your inner child is the vivacious, insatiably curious, and creative part of you. Find something silly that you both love doing together. That may be having pillow fights, blowing bubbles, making art, dancing to music, making cookie dough, playing with your children, or anything that makes you both want to giggle and jump gleefully. Luna and I enjoy chasing, playing with, and cuddling our dog Forest. We've shared so much joy and laughter simply watching his silly antics (and joining in!).

Right now, you might feel a bit of resistance and skepticism to being silly and having fun. But don't worry, many people do. We all have three inner modes of being: the inner child, inner adult, and inner parent. Your inner parent (particularly if you've internalized your own parent's negativity) might feel derisive of anything "immature" or childish. But just be mindful of that part of you, and have fun anyway.

3. Pull a card

In the morning, make a habit out of pulling one card with your partner from an oracle or tarot deck. Discuss the card you each pulled and how its message applies to your inner child work journey.

4. Write your childhood story

Spend some time writing about what your childhood was like alongside your partner. Explore, for instance:

- how you spent your time
- what your parents/caretakers/siblings were like
- what you liked doing
- what you disliked doing
- childhood friends
- your best memories
- your worst memories

Feel free to include as many elements of your childhood as you like or believe to be relevant. When you're done, swap your childhood stories. Read each other's childhood narratives and try to commit them to memory. When you're finished, recount each other's childhoods out loud. Ask if you've understood correctly. By doing this, you're getting to know your partner's inner child better.

5. Shine the light on childhood shadows

On a piece of paper, write down:

(1) what you liked the most about your parents as a child

(2) what you disliked the most about your parents as a child

(3) what scared you the most as a child

(4) what made you feel most comforted as a child

Do this activity with your soul mate or twin flame. Once you're finished, read each other's responses and hold space for any more discussion to occur. This activity will shine the light on potential shadows, traumas, and triggers you both have that originated in childhood. The positive qualities and activities that your inner child enjoyed will reveal what you most need to heal. Discuss what you wrote together.

6. Draw your inner child

Gather some art materials (such as pencils, paint or pens) and four pieces of blank paper. You will be using two pieces, and your partner will be using two pieces. On one of the pages draw an image of your inner child at their happiest. Don't worry if you're not good at drawing – that's not the point of this activity. Just go with whatever first pops into your mind (don't overthink it). On the other page, draw your inner child at their saddest and most wounded. When you're both done, examine your drawings. What themes arise? What colors do you use, and what do they mean to you? Help each other interpret what has been illustrated. After you're both done, write down in your inner work journal what you've discovered. Have you had any epiphanies? Has anything been made clear?

Path 3 – Shadow Work

The final level (or path) of inner work is shadow work. This is a practice that needs to be approached with as much awareness, sensitivity, and compassion as you can muster. Perhaps the best advice here is only to expose yourself to *small doses*. "Why?" you may wonder. The answer is that shadow work can become overwhelming and intensely threatening to the ego very quickly. If you do *too much* shadow work at once (e.g., in one sitting), you may debilitate yourself and also cause your shadow to go into even deeper hiding. Remember that your shadow lurks in the dark corners of your mind for a reason: it has been consciously or unconsciously banished there.

Your shadow represents everything within you that has been deemed flawed, ugly, unworthy, perverse or taboo. Again, I want to emphasize here that your shadow is *not you*, but it is a *part* of you. In other words, it is composed of all fleeting or long-standing thoughts, feelings, habits, preferences, desires, or personality traits that have been shamed at one point or another throughout your life.

It's also essential to mention here the potentially adverse impact shadow work might have on your relationship if you aren't suitably prepared. To be prepared, you must have a solid sense of self, healthy self-esteem, a nurtured and protected inner child and a relationship that is based on implicit trust. When any of these four elements aren't present, all hell can break loose. So this is a fair warning. Shadow work is a sacred process that needs to be approached with respect and slow, mindful deliberation.

With that being said, here are some illuminating ways to practice shadow work with your twin flame or soul mate:

1. Look for the triggers

Pay attention to what triggers you about your partner. A trigger is any strong negative emotional reaction that is out of proportion to the situation. In other words, when someone "overreacts," they are actually getting triggered – and that trigger has its roots in the shadow which is projected (or displaced) onto the other person.

Write down everything that triggers you about your partner on a piece of paper. Ideally, try to keep a record in your personal diary to refer back to later. Encourage your partner to do the same. Once you have recorded each trigger, try to find the underlying wound you carry. For example, if you get intensely angry when your partner interrupts you, look "underneath" this behavior. Don't take it at face value. Try to find what underlying need is not being met (e.g., not being seen or valued) or what childhood wound you may carry (e.g., being dominated by one of your parents). Remember, a trigger isn't a petty annoyance – it is an overreaction to something happening in the present moment. Once you are finished writing down and deconstructing your triggers, share them with your partner, and vice versa. Hold space for each other and have an introspective discussion.

2. Soul gazing

Find a quiet and comfortable place and block out ten to fifteen minutes on your calendar. For this activity, you will be practicing something called soul gazing, which essentially means sitting in front of each other and looking deeply into each other's eyes without talking. Have a pen and paper close by – you will need it after your soul gazing session.

Once you're ready, play some soft atmospheric music in the background to help set the mood. Begin to gaze into each other's eyes softly. If you find your gaze becomes a stare, try to relax it and blink slowly. As you gaze into your partner's eyes pay attention to any thoughts or feelings that arise inside of you. Does anything other than a sense of love arise? Remember, it's okay to have these thoughts and feelings. Don't judge them. Just be aware of them.

After a while, any uncomfortable feelings or thoughts may subside and give way to a deeper soul connection. The eyes are indeed the windows of the soul, and it is common for couples to have spiritual – even mystical – experiences while practicing soul gazing. Gazing into each other's eyes is also a wonderful way to reinforce a strong spiritual bond that transcends the ego. So this practice is two-fold: it can be used as a form of shadow work, but also as a form of light work (or connecting with the Divine).

Whenever Luna and I have done this activity, we've noticed the paranoias and insecurities of the ego arise first as we gaze at each other. But after a few minutes, those shadow barriers fade and give way to a deeper presence, a shared communion of soul-meets-soul. Give yourself time and feel free to stop if the soul gazing becomes too much. Being *truly* seen can be scary, so please know that it's okay to go slowly and stop if it becomes too intense.

3. Identify projections

Projection is what happens when we see our own flaws in another person that we unconsciously refuse to see inside ourselves. This form of emotional displacement makes it much easier to live with ourselves because *everyone else* is responsible for our misery – *not us*! It's also possible to project our strengths onto other people, especially if we've been taught to deny them in childhood. For instance, if we were conditioned to be timid as a child, we may greatly admire others who are outspoken and bold.

In this shadow work practice, you'll need to choose one strength and one weakness in your partner and record it in your journal. Again, this is a practice that can be done by both of you at the same time – so your partner will also pick a strength and weakness of their choosing about you. When you're done, write underneath the strength how it has been denied in you. For instance, if you admire how great an artist your partner is, write about how your father made fun of your drawings as a child, and thus squashed your inner artist.

Next, focus on the weakness apparent in your partner. Beneath it, explore how that *very same* weakness shows up in you. For instance, if you wrote about how insensitive your partner can sometimes be, explore how you are insensitive towards yourself and others. Once you're finished, share your discoveries with each other. This is a practice that can be slowly incorporated into every aspect of your life. The more you're able to catch your projections, the more your shadow will come to light and have the opportunity to be embraced and transformed.

4. Unearth core beliefs

Your core beliefs are the central ideas or convictions you have about yourself. They form the foundation of your ego and dictate how you feel about yourself deep down. Where did core beliefs come from, you might wonder? Our core beliefs were primarily inherited from our parents, teachers, societies, and religious institutions. However, they aren't static, and they can shift and evolve as we progress through life.

What's most important to understand is that core beliefs are the *absolute truths* we believe about ourselves – as such they are often at the root of our suffering. But what do core beliefs sound like? Below you'll find a list of common core beliefs. For this activity, both you and your partner will need to read through the list below quietly and note any feelings that arise while reading through it:

I am bad.

I am stupid.

I am worthless.

I am a loser.

I am unlikeable.

I am unlovable.

I am irredeemably flawed.

I am a failure.

I am weak.

I am not enough.

I don't deserve good things.

I am unworthy of happiness.

I don't matter.

I am boring.

I am crazy and unstable.

I always hurt people.

I can't be fixed.

I always hurt myself.

I have no hope.

I am evil/sinful.

I deserve to be punished.

I am unwanted.

I am invisible.

I am a mistake.

I am helpless.

I am powerless.

I am ugly.

I am shameful.

I will die alone.

You can either read directly from this page, photocopy two copies of this page, or copy down each toxic core belief by hand. Reading off the page is much quicker, but there is an advantage to writing down each core belief by hand: you'll be even more in-tune with how each core belief impacts you. By paying attention to how your body, heart, or mind reacts, you'll be able to unearth the core beliefs that are closest to those you hold.

Is it possible to have more than one core belief? Yes! Look out for strong emotions and thoughts that surge through you while going through the list. It's likely that you'll stumble across more than one core belief (most people do). Also pay attention to any physical signs of shaking, heat, coldness, tension or withholding – these are also indications that you've come across one of your core beliefs. Remember, these sensations may be very subtle, so ensure you're in a quiet and undisturbed place while doing this activity.

You'll also need to do this practice separately from your partner so that you're not influenced by each other's responses. You may wish to mentally note which core beliefs triggered you or circle them with a pencil. If you're sharing this book with your partner, make sure you erase (or delete the highlight if you're reading off a screen) the core beliefs you've marked to provide a clean slate for your beloved.

Once you're finished, discuss your findings together. Explore how you feel and how you think these core beliefs may negatively impact your life and relationship together. After your discussion, you may like to devise some positive affirmations together. Positive affirmations are a dynamic way to rewire core beliefs, particularly when repeated many times during the day. Examples of positive affirmations can include "I am beautiful," "I am worthy," "I am lovable," "I am whole and complete," "I am curious and intelligent," and so forth. Try to phrase your affirmations positively and in the present tense, rather than in the negative or past tense (e.g., "I'm not a failure, I can be successful" is not as empowering as simply saying "I am successful"). Remember, the affirmations you pick may sound cheesy at first, but that's because your mind is conditioned to believe the opposite. The more you repeat the affirmation with conviction, the more it will slowly reprogram your negative conditioning.

5. Draw your shadow self

With your partner, gather two pieces of blank paper and some drawing supplies. Put on some music that you both enjoy, light some candles, and reflect on your shadow self. Is it human? Is it another species? How tall is it? Where does it live inside of you? What colors best suit your shadow self? You might even like to give your shadow self a name if that helps.

Probably the best time to do this activity is at night by candlelight as it helps to prepare the mind and set the mood. (The night time is symbolic of death, darkness, the unconscious, hidden forces, etc.). It's also best to sit away from your partner so that you're not influenced by what they draw, and vice versa.

It must be emphasized that drawing your shadow is largely an intuitive activity. Try not to overthink things. Your shadow is rather like a shapeshifter: it can appear in many forms. You're just capturing the current form your shadow has decided to take. Also, it doesn't matter whether you're good at drawing or not – that's not the point of this activity. The point is to help you come 'face-to-face' with your shadow – and also meet your partner's shadow.

Once you're both done, take some time to discuss and reflect on what you've both drawn. How does it make you feel? Keep the pictures you've both drawn and use them in the rest of your inner work practice. For example, you may like to use your shadow self picture as a basis for meditation, a journaling session, or a visualization.

6. Go on an inner journey

The phrase 'inner journey' may sound daunting and long-winded, but it doesn't have to be. Inner journeying can take anywhere from ten minutes to an hour or more. It's up to you and your soul mate/twin flame to decide how much time you want to designate. But obviously, the more time you take to relax your mind and enter into a mild altered state of consciousness, the more powerful the experience will be.

To enter an altered state of consciousness, try meditation, chanting, dancing, listening to music or anything that greatly relaxes you. In this activity, you'll both be meeting your shadow selves and retrieving crucial information about your relationship.

To begin, find a quiet, preferably dark, and undisturbed place. After you've entered a mild altered state of consciousness and feel very relaxed (e.g., through meditation), lie down and put a blindfold on. You may then either memorize or record the following inner journey:

You are in a summery meadow staring at an ancient forest ahead. Slowly you make your way toward the forest. As you reach it, you find an old lamp lying on the ground emanating bright white light. You pick it up and carry it with you, grateful. Entering the forest, you observe how the trees loom, sway, and creak over you. A mysterious pearlescent mist circles around the trees and obscures the distance. The deeper you move into the forest, the darker it gets. But you have a lamp with you, and your spirit guides, ancestors, angels or soul are watching over you. You are safe. But you don't know where you're going. The trees become dark silhouettes around you. Anything could be lurking behind those trees — but even so, you feel calm, strong, and ready to meet whatever is coming. With every step you take the fog becomes denser. It's tendrils snake around your body until your entire vision becomes grey and foggy. Suddenly, you sense a dark presence ahead. You keep walking with your lamp held out in front of you. Slowly the fog begins to subside. A figure emerges. It's your shadow self. You smile gently and say, "welcome, I've been longing to meet you." Your shadow responds and keeps its distance as the light in your lamp is too strong. A question bubbles up inside of you as you take in the form of your shadow self. "Tell me dear shadow, what do you wish to communicate right now?" You wait for your shadow to respond ... Once your shadow self has finished, you ask another question, "Tell me dear shadow, in what ways do you negatively impact my relationship?" You wait for your shadow to respond ... Once your shadow has finished, you ask any more burning questions on your mind ... Finally, you thank your shadow and bid it goodbye. Immediately, your shadow dissipates, as though it was a vapor of mist itself. You turn around and make your way back to the summery meadow which can be glimpsed through the trees ahead. Once you reach the meadow, you put the lamp down at the meeting point between the meadow and the forest. You know that any time, you can return to this place, pick up the lamp, and find your shadow. The power is in your hands ... Once you put down the lamp, you begin to return to ordinary consciousness. You might wiggle your fingers and toes or do a big stretch and then take off your blindfold. You've now completed the inner journey.

Upon finishing, it's best to immediately record the key points of what happened in a journal so that you don't forget anything. Once you're finished, you can then discuss what happened with your partner.

Remember, it's okay if you didn't get much information the first time. Inner journeys sometimes take a while for us to warm up to. Also, if you find that any part of this journey gets too overwhelming at any point, you're free to stop, get up, practice self-love, and do something different.

Often, the answers we receive from our shadow selves are symbolic, cryptic or scrambled. They may take some time, reflection, and meditation to decipher and fully understand. So don't expect to necessarily get a clear understanding of yourself or your relationship straight away. Also, keep in mind that the answers your shadow may have given might be warped or blown out of proportion. Listen to your intuition and gut instincts and don't be afraid to ask for further clarification from your soul or spirit guides.

Likely, this journey would have given you some interesting information to ponder. Discuss with your partner what your shadow revealed about its influence on the relationship. As always, do this mindfully, slowly, and gently. Create a safe space to explore what is revealed.

Finally, don't forget to finish the practice with a supportive hug or kiss. This work can be deep and heavy, and it is courageous of the two of you to undertake it. The work you're doing together is rare, powerful, and life-changing. By committing to it, you are committing to the evolution of consciousness itself and the awakening of humanity as a whole. What you do creates an unfathomable number of ripple effects in the world around you. So thank you for being brave and doing the work.

Spiritual Partnerships and Other-Transformation

When you commit to a spiritual partnership with another human being, you bring the energy of the archetype of spiritual partnership into the physical arena. You begin to form and to live by the values, perceptions, and actions that reflect equality with your partner and a commitment to his or her spiritual development and your own. You begin to set aside the wants of your personality in order to accommodate the needs of your partner's spiritual growth, and, in doing that, you grow yourself. That is how spiritual partnership works.

– GARY ZUKAV

We've just explored how you can experience personal transformation and spiritual metamorphosis in conjunction with your partner. But what about exclusively helping *your partner* to grow and evolve? As Zukav pointed out above, spiritual partnerships are just as much about committing to the growth of your partner as to your own growth.

There is a certain inexplicable beauty and delight in watching the spiritual metamorphosis of a person we love. The paradox is that by helping our partner to grow, we indirectly help ourselves to grow. But here, the emphasis must be on our partner, on the *other*.

We have a tendency in this era to be very self-absorbed and self-serving, particularly when it comes to our self-growth and healing in life. But the qualities of altruism, generosity, compassion, and attentiveness to others' needs must all be developed on the spiritual path. By taking care of our loved ones, we take care of ourselves and the world around us while developing these sacred qualities.

We all need to feel held, supported, and protected within a relationship. Your partner has wounds and traumas that are just as real and painful as yours. By helping and looking out for them, you are facilitating their awakening process. What could be more precious than that?

If you'd like to know how to aid your partner's awakening journey, you'll find some guidance below. For the sake of brevity and clarity, I've put these into numbered bullet points. But keep in mind that each point can take months, even years to master. Even so, you can practice these at any stage of your soul mate or twin flame partnership:

1. *Practice active listening.* Try not to interrupt your partner or impose your thoughts/beliefs onto them. Simply receive what they have to say patiently. This will help your partner to feel seen, heard and understood.

2. *Understand your partner's triggers.* What makes them feel unsafe? What triggers unpleasant childhood memories? What provokes the negative core beliefs within them? Pay close attention to when your partner overreacts and ask yourself, "What is their unmet need in this situation?" If you're not sure, ask your partner what they need. They might give you an unrealistic, angry, or sarcastic response due to being riled up, but try not to take this personally. Find the unmet needs underneath. Remember that our deepest needs are to feel safe, loved, and accepted.

3. *Motivate them.* Not everyone likes or enjoys inner work. If your partner struggles to get started or seems to be neglecting their spiritual growth, try motivating them (in a non-pressuring way). Even better, set the example and invite them to come and meditate with you in the morning or practice something else like inner child work. Use words of affirmation and praise when the situation feels right ("I'm so proud of you!" "You're doing great").

4. *Provide a safe place.* One of the most essential skills you can develop in a spiritual partnership is the quality of openness and non-judgment. Your partner needs to feel safe, particularly during challenging forms of inner work like shadow work. You may like to practice suspending your judgment with other people in your life to hone these abilities. Remember, a person feels safe when they are seen, heard, and validated.

5. *Help prevent spiritual burnout.* Spiritual burnout happens when we're doing too much inner work too quickly. Signs of burnout may include becoming moody, withdrawn, overridden with grief, shame, anxiety, chronic physical illness, or anything that suggests your partner is emotionally, mentally, or physically struggling. However, with that being said, feeling and working through the pain we carry is often part of the journey of healing – and can be confused with spiritual burnout. Try to make the distinction between spiritual burnout and the integration process by talking with your partner. What do they need the most at the moment? If appropriate, suggest doing something fun and unrelated to spiritual work such as cooking, gardening or going to see a movie.

6. *Help prevent spiritual bypassing.* Spiritual bypassing is the phenomenon of using spiritual practice to avoid, suppress, or escape from uncomfortable issues in life. Have you ever observed "spiritual" types of people talk a lot about "love and light" and "vibrating higher" – but completely avoid (or reject) anything remotely negative or real? This is the essence of spiritual bypassing. When we spiritually bypass, we use spirituality as a crutch to avoid whatever makes us feel uncomfortable. The best way to prevent spiritual bypassing is to practice shadow work. If you notice your soul mate or twin flame misusing spirituality, the best thing to do might be to discuss your own shadow work discoveries. By normalizing the shadow, you'll help them to go deeper into their spiritual practice.

7. *Give them space.* Often the spiritual journey requires a great deal of silence, introspection, and solitude. If your partner feels more distant, ask if they need space. Likely, they will appreciate your attentiveness and explain what they need (e.g., time to journal, space to meditate, alone time in nature). Recognize that at times you will both need to stand far apart from each other, and that's okay. A cocoon can only hold one caterpillar. If your lives are

both hectic, discuss the possibility of scheduling alone time into your days.

Often, when it comes to supporting your partner's spiritual transformation, all that is needed is to be receptive and hold space. Getting too involved (which can be perceived as being naggy, pressuring or domineering) is often not required. When you *do* need to take a more active role, do it subtly and gently and always strive for a two-way conversation.

Spiritual Partnerships and World Transformation

Finally, we come to using our spiritual partnerships as a way of catalyzing world transformation. This may sound rather audacious, but as mentioned earlier in this chapter, when soul mates and twin flames unite, the energy they project into this world is intense – particularly when there is a shared purpose or vision.

In order to send ripples of change into the world and fulfill the destiny of soul mate and twin flame relationships, there needs to be a starting place. Positively improving the lives of hundreds, even thousands of people is no small task. A lot of preparation, inner work, and soul searching needs to be done first.

As you may or may not already be aware, Luna and I are passionate about the topic of worldwide transformation. Since the initiation of our relationship on the 11th of November, 2011, we have created a popular spiritual website, designed numerous free courses, written books, published journals, and offered various other services. Our journey hasn't been easy, and it has had its fair share of hiccups, chaos, and confusion, but we share a unified vision of helping people spiritually awaken. And it is that shared vision that drives and gives us meaning each day. In fact, by fulfilling this shared vision, we believe we are fulfilling our personal life purposes. It is a tremendous blessing to be able to experience that with someone you love.

Back in 2011, we knew nothing of the twin flame concept and had no idea that our relationship would be the birth ground of so much positive work and change. But there was an urge within us to unite forces and *create* something big. You might feel the very same urge deep down, and it's because you have a larger life mission.

Do all soul mates and twin flames have to share the same unified vision? No, not necessarily. Sometimes we find ourselves with a unique purpose that only we must fulfill. Alternatively, we might find ourselves in a position of helping our partners fulfill their life purpose (which becomes *our* life purpose). There are no black or white rules here.

However, if you do feel that your relationship is destined to fulfill a larger unified mission, you'll benefit from the following points of advice:

1. Create an autonomous spiritual practice

When relationships are not approached consciously, they are used to play out endless levels of codependency and attachment. But as we've explored previously in this book, we don't need anyone else, *even a twin flame or soul mate,* to make us whole because the truth is that we are innately whole at a soul level.

A big part of maintaining this sense of self-sovereignty and autonomy within your relationship is creating a separate spiritual practice from your partner that does not require their participation. This practice will ideally be a daily commitment, but will ultimately be fit around your needs.

While it's important to do *some* of your spiritual practice with your soul mate or twin flame, the majority needs to be done autonomously – or solo. Why? The answer is that inner work is exclusively to do with *you* and exploring *your own* inner landscape. While it's important to motivate and inspire each other in your relationship, ultimately this path must be done alone. You cannot do the work for your partner, and vice versa – nor should you need to.

By committing to a spiritual practice each day, you are demonstrating true sincerity and self-responsibility. Be careful of using your relationship as a crutch or a way to avoid committing to inner work and self-transformation. To truly go deep, you'll need the privacy of solitude and introspection. The more you grow, the stronger and more self-contained you'll be in your relationship. If both of you are overly relying on each other to get your spiritual sustenance, the foundation that you build will be weak. What would happen, for instance, if a crisis (say the death of a mother or father) came along? Who would support who?

The more you are committed to individually growing together, the easier it will be to hold space and provide stability and safety within your relationship. When no one is "tending their own lawn" there is chaos and uncertainty. Furthermore, by creating an independent spiritual practice, you will be strengthening yourself (and therefore your relationship) to endure the pressures of creating big changes in the world. World transformation is impossible without self-transformation – and self-transformation is primarily a solitary practice.

2. Authenticity

How is it possible to inspire genuine, positive changes in this world if we aren't being true to ourselves? How is it possible to achieve our ultimate life purpose if we're solely putting something out there that we think *others* will like?

Authenticity sounds simple in theory but is much harder in practice. To be authentic, we must stand firm in who we are and respect our needs, desires, beliefs, and values. But in a world full of noisy and clashing demands, opinions, and expectations from others, that can be hard! It's so easy to lose touch with the voice of our soul and become people-pleasers, or worse, sell outs who are invested in nothing but earning more money.

Thankfully, in soul mate and twin flame relationships, we have a living mirror who will show us the truth of our behavior (intentionally or unintentionally). Whether we like it or not, our beliefs, mindsets, habits, and shadows will be illuminated and put on display for us to see clearly. We may observe our pretense and fakery through the behavior of our partner (who is directly influenced by us), or we may clash with our partner and continuously come up against roadblock after roadblock. Whatever the case, we *will* eventually be forced to walk authentically. But whether we go willingly or grudgingly is a whole other matter.

But authenticity isn't only confined to the realms of creativity, it's also a core component of successful twin flame and soul mate relationships. As Mark Nepo writes, "Unconditional love is not so much about how we receive and endure each other, as it is about the deep vow to never, under any condition, stop bringing the flawed truth of who we are to each other."

In order to create real change in the world, it is vital that we are honest and transparent with our partners. Lying, pretending, and playing games will not only create suffering in the relationship but will distract from our ability to achieve the ultimate purpose of spiritual partnerships: to create worldwide transformation. As such, learning to speak openly, admit shortcomings, and practice forgiveness will be vital. Without these practices, without being honest with each other, the relationship will weaken and disintegrate into petty psychological games that achieve nothing.

Remember, if you don't feel safe being authentic with your partner, it's worth exploring why and making that the utmost priority. All soul mate and twin flame relationships are characterized by authenticity, and when that element is missing, no true love, respect, or growth can happen.

3. Discover your shared values, dreams, and complementing strengths

Depending on how well the two of you know yourselves, discovering your shared values, dreams, and complementing strengths can take some time. In our case, it took about seven years! So don't be disheartened if you don't make much progress straight away. Not only must you understand yourself deeply, but you must also understand where exactly the two of you *overlap* – and that is no small task. After all, our twin flames and soul mates are often very different people from us!

It's best to truly and deeply know yourself first before you attempt to find where the two of you overlap. The best place to start is of course with some vigorous soul-searching. Begin by exploring your authentic values and strengths. Reflect on the following question: *if everything was taken away from you, what would remain inside of you?*

The soul-searching process is not always a straightforward path. Be aware that sometimes deceptions are masquerading as truths, and truths are masquerading as deceptions. Doing this work can certainly feel like you're walking into a house of mirrors! For instance, you might discover something marvelous about yourself, but later find it was a smokescreen of lies that temporarily hypnotized you into a state of ego-inflated grandiosity. Or you might be told by a spiritual guide of some kind that you possess a specific gift, but later discover that the gift you possess is much greater (and much more different) than you initially thought.

Also, sometimes what we think is *ours* is actually an inherited form of conditioning from our parents or society. The same goes for the dreams and strengths we carry – we must be able to untangle ourselves from the web of inherited voices within us to see the truth. Sometimes, this task can take years depending on how deep and complex our conditioning has been.

Once you've stripped away the beliefs, values, and various other forms of brainwashing you've absorbed through life and have met your core essence, it's time to practice some spiritual alchemy. What do I mean by spiritual alchemy? In this context, spiritual alchemy is the process of uniting two souls (yourself and your partner's) to create one beautiful metaphorical love child (the Philosopher's Stone or alchemical gold). This can be a simple task or an exceptionally difficult one. Also, there is no set formula so the process will be unique to you and your partner. However, there are a few suggestions you may like to explore. I'll briefly list them below:

- Create a mindmap and explore your shared values, dreams, and strengths
- Draw a Venn diagram and write your contrasting strengths/weaknesses, and in the middle your shared strengths/weaknesses
- Consult your dreams and look for symbolic signs/answers
- Visualize your big-picture goals together (make use of the law of attraction) and observe what opportunities Life puts in front of you
- Go on an inner journey (sober) or shamanic journey (using plant medicine)
- Find and use thought-provoking questions that shift your perspectives and help you both to uncover some interesting answers (a couple of examples include: "From the perspective of your deathbed, what would you be most happy to have achieved?" and "Identify three core insecurities holding you back")

- Request the guidance of your soul, spirit guides, ancestors, etc.

Of course, this is not an exhaustive list, and there are many other techniques you can employ to find your shared life purpose. But hopefully, the above ideas serve as a springboard for you to form your own.

The Power of Spiritual Partnerships

It is an extraordinarily strange thing to be alive in these times. We are at a point in history where we are facing the genuine possibility of large scale destruction, extinction, and a multitude of other catastrophic effects that arise as our planet is plunged into the chaos of climate change. As we witness these impacts, the danger becomes more real, and the need to awaken and create change is more needed than ever before.

As the destruction of our great Mother Earth bleeds into our own lives and as industrialization gnaws into our bones and feeds our existential emptiness, we are desperately searching for something. Getting a job, getting married, having kids, and contributing to the great Materialistic Machine until we die no longer fulfills us. We need something more. We need to create a legacy, something of substance, something that will actually catalyze long-lasting positive change in the world.

This is where the promise of spiritual partnerships comes in. Unlike traditional marriages that are committed to material safety and comfort, the spiritual partnership goes one step further and makes a commitment to mutual spiritual growth. Within spiritual partnerships, the focus is not just on *us,* our needs, our desires, and our petty grievances – instead, the focus gradually becomes local, national, and global. Furthermore, in spiritual partnerships the relationship isn't just biologically fulfilled when having a child, it becomes spiritually fulfilled when giving birth to a *spiritual child* – a shared vision.

As clinical psychologist John Welwood writes, "Further, as a man and woman become devoted to the growth of awareness and spirit in each other, they will naturally want to share their love with others. The new qualities they give birth to, generosity, courage, compassion, wisdom, can extend beyond the circle of their own relationship. These qualities are a couples "Spiritual Child" – what their coming together gives to the world. A couple will flourish when their vision and practice are not focused solely on each other, but also include this larger sense of community and what they can give to others."

This spiritual child can take numerous forms, but perhaps what is most powerful about it is its ability to generate personal and large-scale transformation. Again, to use the analogy mentioned earlier in this chapter: one person alone is like a lighthouse. But two people together become like a laser beam. When we are in a spiritual partnership, we have the sacred opportunity and responsibility to bring this dynamic force of change to the world.

What Next? (Concluding Thoughts)

Now that you've reached the end of this book you might be wondering, what's next? You've learned about soul mates and twin flames, how to distinguish between them, how to find them, how to identify harmful myths and toxic shadows, how to move through separation and grief, and how to use your relationship to achieve a higher purpose. You've been educated about the essential tools and practices needed to foster a healthy, awakened partnership. But where do you start?

As we have mentioned previously, this is a book to be *lived* not just read. The best thing to do next is to think about your biggest need right now. Where is there a gap in your life? Where is more work needed? For example, if you're struggling through a twin flame separation, revisit Chapter 9, meditate on what's written, and put it into practice. If you're unsure about how healthy your relationship is, revisit Chapter 8. If you simply want to know how to improve your twin flame or soul mate relationship, see Chapter 11 and explore the different kinds of inner work.

This is not a book that has been created to be read and discarded – it has been designed to be a reference book that you consult over and over again. After all, we believe that what has been transmitted through this book is a *collective* effort, a channeling of the Universal Mind that understands the dire state of the planet and what is needed to create large-scale change. Thanks to the thousands of heartfelt stories and lessons of trial, error, and hard-earned wisdom shared with us, this book has appeared before you. We sincerely hope it has been of help and continues to inspire you.

To conclude, we'll leave you with a beautiful quote by the Sufi mystic Rumi that summarizes the divine message at the core of soul mate and twin flame union:

The minute I heard my first love story,
I started looking for you,
not knowing how blind that was.
Lovers don't finally meet somewhere.
They're in each other all along.

APPENDIX 1

Q&A

If you still have a few lingering questions regarding twin flame and soul mate relationships, you may like to read this section. Here are our responses to some of the most commonly asked questions regarding twin flame and soul mate relationships:

Q. How can I help my twin flame/soul mate awaken?

A. The best way is by leading through example. Let your own commitment to self-growth and spiritual transformation inspire them. Remember, it's not your responsibility to awaken your twin flame or soul mate – that's *their* responsibility. Trying to force them to awaken will not only repel them and send them the message that "they're not good enough," but it also tries to deprive them of their own power to create change. Leave the power in their hands. When their soul is ready to awaken, it will awaken.

Leading by example is a passive way of helping your soul mate/twin flame find the way.

Q. Does everyone have a twin flame?

A. Yes, it's quite likely that everyone has a twin flame. But not everyone can connect with their twin flame within this lifetime. Twin flames emerge within our lives when our souls are ready to undergo the process of spiritual awakening and transformation. For some people, the twin flame connection is simply too intense and is not welcome, and hence never happens.

Q. Is it possible to have a twin flame/soul mate who doesn't believe in the twin flame/soul mate concept?

A. Yes, it is possible. Remember that the twin flame concept is a framework or story that is created by the mind to understand reality. Love is beyond labels and words, but on a human level, we need to label our relationships to understand them. So it is possible that you're both in a twin flame/soul mate relationship without your partner actually believing in those terms.

Q. Does everyone have a soul mate?

A. Yes, we all have at least one soul mate on this earth right now. However, not all of us are open to the possibility of connecting with our soul mate due to negative beliefs, self-destructive habits, and other limiting patterns of behavior. Unfortunately, some people are programmed with the belief that they're not "worthy" of happiness or aren't "good enough." Often, those who do inner work find that they're able to connect with their soul mate finally after years of searching.

Q. Can a twin flame be a soul mate?

A. Yes, it is possible that a soul mate can become a twin flame and vice versa. But twin flames and soul mates have different functions. Twin flame relationships are intense and challenging: their purpose is to help you spiritually grow. Soul mate relationships, on the other hand, are more mild and peaceful: their purpose is to help support you. It's like the difference between fire (twin flames) and water (soul mates).

Q. Is a twin flame one soul split into two bodies?

A. That is a matter of opinion. Personally, we believe that twin flames are souls that have decided to reincarnate with each other across many lifetimes for the purpose of mutual spiritual illumination. Like biological twins, twin flames are 'birthed' into this world by Spirit and have very similar DNA (or soul energy) but not exactly the same.

When we look at biological twins, they start as one single embryo that splits into two parts, and from then on, the DNA begins diverging. We believe the same for twin flames: they both originate from the same Source, but their souls are whole and complete unto themselves. As mentioned earlier in this book (see Chapter 10), the belief that our flames complete us opens the door to immense suffering. As such, we don't believe that twin flames are "the missing parts" of each other. Instead, they are the catalysts of tremendous spiritual growth and evolution.

Q. Why do twin flames run?

A. Sometimes, our twin flames run away because the connection is too overwhelming and intense for the ego. When the ego is not ready to spiritually evolve, it resists, fights, and tries to escape – this is why twin flames run and try to avoid the relationship.

Q. Do we only have one twin flame?

A. Yes, there is only one other person on the planet who can be called a twin flame (as the name "twin" implies). All types of relationships provide the opportunity for growth, but twin flame relationships are rare in their ability to help us spiritually evolve and awaken.

Q. Do we only have one soul mate?

A. No. Many people (including the two of us) believe that we have many soul mates who exist in a multitude of forms. Our soul mates can be our partners, friends, coworkers, siblings, or even animal companions. One thing is for sure: all the soul mates we meet throughout our lives will have a major impact on us. Our lives will be much richer after coming into contact with these souls.

Q. Can twin flames or soul mates fall out of love?

A. Yes, unfortunately, it is possible for twin flames and soul mates to fall out of love. However, this is not to say that the deep soul connection will disappear, or the possibility for rekindling love will vanish. It is possible for twin flames/soul mates to fall in love, fall out of love, and fall in love again. The nature of life is unpredictable, and there is no divine edict saying that twin flames or soul mates must love each other for an entire lifetime. The purpose of twin flame and soul mate relationships is to support us on our spiritual path of transformation, and when that goal has been completed, the connection can sometimes disintegrate. However, it is always possible for our twin flames or soul mates to re-emerge later in life. Also keep in mind that "falling out of love" is very ego-based – but on a spiritual level, twin flames and soul mates will always be in love as their true essence *is*

Love. So while it's possible to fall out of love on an ego level, it's not possible to fall out of love on the Spirit level.

Q. Is there such a thing as a false twin flame?

A. Yes, there is such a thing as a false twin flame (and also false soul mate!). Whether due to our own warped perception (it's true that love blinds us) or due to the pretense worn by the other person, it's possible to mistake someone as our twin flame. The best way to know whether someone is a false twin flame is to pay attention to (a) whether they genuinely share the same values as you, (b) if you can be your true self around them, and (c) if there is mutual spiritual transformation.

Q. Is love at first sight real?

A. Yes, we personally believe that love at first sight is real. Souls can and do recognize each other very quickly. But don't confuse love at first sight with romantic projection or delusion (please see Chapter 10 for more on this). It is possible to fall in love with your *idea* of a person – not the person as they *actually are.* It is also possible to project your romantic hopes and dreams onto a person and believe they feel the same way, when in reality they don't. Always try your best to verify how the other person feels toward you so your heart isn't wounded.

Q. Can a soul mate or twin flame hurt you?

A. Yes, it is possible for a soul mate or twin flame to hurt you. No relationship is perfect, and arguments, as well as emotional hurt, can occur in any type of relationship. However, in soul mate/twin flame relationships, your partner won't intentionally try to harm you. More often than not they *unintentionally* harm you as a result of their own unresolved wounds.

Q. Why won't my twin flame or soul mate talk to me?

A. There are a number of reasons why your twin flame or soul mate may be giving you the silent treatment. First, if you have been in a relationship with each other and your partner suddenly stops talking to you, it may be because the connection is too intense for their ego to handle. Something deep within them (such as a core fear or wound) may have been triggered and suddenly risen to the surface without warning. In this case, they may need space and time to process what is happening, alone. This may be alarming to you, particularly if you didn't do or say anything that would elicit such an extreme reaction. As painful as it is, try to understand that this is a natural part of the growth process. The more you try to push them into contacting you, the more pressured they will feel, and the more likely they will resist contact for even longer.

Another possibility is that you haven't known the person (who you interpret as being your soul mate/twin flame) for very long and have got a little over-enthusiastic in contacting them. This display of intensity may spook the person, particularly if they're wanting to go slow and see what the relationship evolves into. In this case, it would be better to slow down the communication and channel the intense enthusiasm in another way (such as through exercise or creativity). Allow the person to contact you in their own time and clarify what the relationship means to them so that you're both on the same page (after you've made it clear that you're interested in them).

The third possibility is that the person is a false twin flame or soul mate. They may simply not be interested in you and so are keeping their distance. Remember, if they don't share the same values as you, if you don't feel the freedom to be your true self, and if you haven't undergone any spiritual transformation while with them, they are likely not your true soul mate or twin flame.

Q. Can twin flames communicate telepathically?

A. Yes, it might be possible for twin flames to communicate telepathically when in a relationship. But this shouldn't be used as an excuse to avoid clear communication and assume that the other can 'read our mind.' Telepathic communication can also lead a person to believe they are reading another person's emotions and thoughts accurately, when in reality they are projecting their own beliefs, wishes and desires onto that person. This is a tricky area and should be approached with open-minded caution. But attempting to send love telepathically to our twin flames is always a positive and nourishing practice (it can be compared to the Tibetan Buddhist *Metta* practice or loving-kindness meditation).

Q. I'm not sure if I'm with my twin flame/soul mate. How can I know for sure?

A. This is a common concern, so don't worry, you're not alone. Unfortunately, many people fall into the trap of projecting their desires onto people in their lives whom they feel strong romantic (but not spiritual) attraction toward. They may mislabel these people as their twin flames or soul mates, and in a sort of romantic delusion, ignore the signs that the person they're with is simply not a great fit for them. Thankfully, since you're asking this question, you haven't yet been swept off into romantic delusion. The easiest answer is to give your relationship time and space to evolve. It's not always easy to understand the true nature of our relationships when they are first established as the ecstacy of new love can blind us. If you like, you can always take the test in Appendix 2 and 3 to determine what type of relationship you might have – but take the result you receive as a possibility, not a certainty. In truth, the only way to be sure that you're with your twin flame or soul mate is to let time pass and see how the relationship unfolds. For example, do you both share the same spiritual goals and values? Are you challenged to grow and transform mentally, emotionally, and spiritually? You might also like to ask your higher powers (e.g., Soul, Spirit Guides, Ancestors, etc.) for guidance. But be mindful of confirmation bias (aka., seeing what we *want* to see, not what truly is there).

Q. Are twin flames and soul mates meant to be lovers?

A. No, not necessarily. There is no such thing as a cookie-cutter twin flame or soul mate relationship. Some are lovers, while some are best friends. You don't have to feel sexually attracted to your twin flame or soul mate for the connection to be legitimate. It's perfectly normal to have a platonic relationship.

Q. I keep seeing 11:11. Does that mean I've found my twin flame or soul mate?

A. It might. According to numerology, the number 11 is a "master number" which signifies intuition, insight, and enlightenment. When paired together, 11:11 is a clear message from the universe to become conscious and aware. Many people suggest that seeing 11:11 signifies that your spirit guides are attempting to contact you. In my experience, 11:11 seems to be the number of spiritual awakening, signifying that you are on the right path and your actions are aligned with your soul's purpose. In other words, seeing 11:11 is a good sign! An energetic doorway is being opened in which you will experience spiritual growth. Whether this is through uniting with your twin flame or soul mate is up to your intuition to decide. Seeing 11:11 isn't the only form of synchronicity out there, so look out for other signs. If you desperately need clarification, try consulting your dreams, soul, spirit guides, or oracle/tarot cards if you have any.

APPENDIX 2

Soul Mate Test

The following test has been created to help you determine what type of soul mate relationship you may be in. There are four main types of soul mates in total. Discovering what kind of soul mate you have will help you to uncover the many emotional, psychological and spiritual gifts inherent in your relationship. Please note that we have chosen to use the term "partner" often in this test. However, soul mate relationships can be completely platonic as well.

Please either note down on a piece of paper or highlight your responses. At the end of this test, you'll be able to calculate your result:

1. When life gets tough, you can always rely on your partner to ...

a) Comfort you.

b) Give you tough love so you don't start pitying yourself.

c) Empathize with you.

d) Help guide you.

2. When you both have a fight, it is …

a) Minor and unserious.

b) Angry and petty.

c) Emotionally charged.

d) Deeply upsetting.

3. What interests do you both mainly share?

a) The same personality type, likes, tastes and sense of humor.

b) Not many – you are attracted to each other because you're both so different.

c) The same beliefs and aspirations.

d) The same values, dreams, and life goals.

4. What annoys you the most about your partner?

a) They are too much like you!

b) They have a habit of pushing your "hot buttons."

c) They are so good to you that it makes you feel bad for getting annoyed at them.

d) They are so in sync with you that they can "see right through" you.

5. The most amazing thing about this person is that ...

a) They are the best friend you have ever had.

b) They have taught you so many important lessons.

c) They are extremely loyal and are always there for you.

d) They have helped you to become the very best version of yourself.

6. Pick one word that best describes your relationship.

a) Harmonious.

b) Testing.

c) Peaceful.

d) Deep.

7. How open can you be with your partner?

a) Pretty open (but I still keep things back).

b) I can sometimes be open (but I'm worried about being judged or hurt).

c) Very open (I share almost everything).

d) Relentlessly open (I hold nothing back).

8. Pick a combination of elements that reflects your relationship energy. (If you don't know much about what each element symbolizes, skip this question.)

a) Earth + Air.

b) Fire + Air.

c) Water + Earth.

d) Ether + Fire.

9. What strange experience/s do you both share?

a) We frequently finish each other's sentences.

b) We share pretty normal, but sweet, experiences.

c) We can read each other's thoughts.

d) We've experienced a lot of synchronicity (e.g., precognition, déjà vu, shared birth signs).

Now it's time to calculate your scores!

If you chose mostly (a) you have a soul friend!

You and your partner are on the same wavelength; you both share the same likes, tastes, values, interests, and goals. Like a best friend, you can count on your partner to comfort you in times of need, and you are so much like each other that your relationship flows smoothly. Soul Friends lovingly share this life journey with us and make the experience so much more enjoyable.

If you chose mostly (b) you have a soul teacher!

Soul Teachers help us to learn important lessons in life both intentionally and often unintentionally. If your partner is a Soul Teacher they might have the tendency of creating challenging (but ultimately beneficial) situations in your life that help you to grow as a person. Although they don't hesitate to push your hot buttons, Soul Teachers are honest and powerful catalysts of change in your life. While being challenged can be unsettling and uncomfortable, Soul Teachers usually help your life journey become rich, empowered and transformative.

If you chose mostly (c) you have a soul companion!

Soul Companions share both attributes of Soul Friends and Soul Teachers: they have a similar personality to ours, but also help to teach, guide, and support us. Unlike Soul Teacher relationships, Soul Companions rarely experience much friction and can coexist together harmoniously. Usually, in Soul Companionship connections, both partners have a similar level of mental, emotional, and spiritual maturity making life an exciting adventure full of learning and discovering things together. The degree of kinship, good humor, and joy experienced between Soul Companions is nourishing to the soul.

If you chose mostly (d) you have a soul mate!

Soul Mates help us to learn, grow and live life to the fullest. If your partner is a Soul Mate, you may feel as though you have known them for centuries, or even from many past lives. Your connection can only be described as deep, harmonious and understanding, and you both have a profound understanding of each other that transcends the superficial personality. In your relationship, there is real authenticity that makes it easy for the two of you to reach your fullest potential. Soul Mates help your life journey become centered, compassionate, and deeply fulfilling.

Also, it's normal to have a partner who is both a Soul Friend and a Soul Teacher, Soul Companion and Soul Mate, and so forth. So examine what answers you chose, both primarily and secondarily.

Please see Chapter 2 for a breakdown of each soul connection if you would like more information.

APPENDIX 3

Twin Flame Test

Twin flames are our mirrors. They reflect back to us our every strength, insecurity, weakness, and shadow element. The purpose of the twin flame relationship is to help us undergo the process of spiritual transformation and become the best version of ourselves possible.

Have you found your twin flame? This test might help. Do take this test with a "grain of salt," however. It has been designed as a fun way to reach some clarity – not to give a set-in-stone diagnosis of your relationship.

Remember to either note down on a piece of paper or highlight your responses. At the end of this test, you'll be able to calculate your result:

1. You're free to be authentically yourself without fear around them:

    a)   Definitely

b) Sometimes I do

c) Not really

2. You feel that you have always somehow "known" this person.

a) Agree

b) Not sure

c) Disagree

3. You feel as though you have been waiting for this person your entire life.

a) Yes!

b) I might feel that way ...

c) No, I feel something different

4. This person is your best friend, muse, teacher, and lover all at the same time:

a) Yes, all of these roles

b) Some of these roles, but not all of them

c) One of these roles, yes

5. The moment you met, you experienced an immediately intense connection with them:

a) Yes, it was quite memorable

b) I'm unsure

c) The connection built gradually

6. You both feel drawn towards the same higher calling or life purpose:

a) I agree, we are

b) Similar, but not the same

c) We are called towards different pursuits

7. How would you describe your arguments/fights:

a) Sometimes we fight, and when we do it's intensely triggering and we try to work through our issues together

b) Our fights are either loud and explosive or silent and bitter

c) We have never really had any arguments or fights

8. Even though you're in a relationship with them, you don't feel "trapped" by them – you feel free:

a) I agree

b) Not sure

c) I sometimes feel trapped

9. How would you describe the energy of attraction you feel around this person?

a) Magnetic and intense

b) Gentle and firm

c) Erotic and exciting

10. Your entire life has been re-examined and rebuilt from the ground up since meeting this person:

a) I agree

b) It might have

c) My life has remained the same, but improved slightly

11. You both can easily read each other's thoughts and emotional energy:

a) Very much so

b) On occasion we can

c) We're still working on that

It's now time to calculate your scores!

If you chose mostly (a) you most likely have found your twin flame!

What a tremendous blessing. You are both like two sides of the same coin: you compliment each other's strengths, weaknesses, light and dark sides perfectly. Your twin flame is someone who you completely trust and feel a sense of inner expansion around. Your life may have changed drastically since meeting your twin flame, and you can't help but feel that this person has inspired you to become better as a whole. And although you both tend to mirror each other's unresolved wounds, sometimes leading to conflict, you both accept each other unconditionally. Deep down, you feel that you have known this person for eternity, and you both share the same spiritual calling.

If you chose mostly (b) you <u>might</u> have found your twin flame.

Your answers indicate that you might have found your twin flame, but unfortunately, we can't give you a definite answer. Some of your answers indicate that you have found your twin flame and other answers that you gave suggest that you haven't. We recommend tuning into your inner feelings and asking yourself, "Does this person make me feel loved, accepted, respected, and help me to grow … or do they make me feel unhappy, neglected, disrespected, and hinder my growth?" In other words, do you feel a sense of freedom and happiness around this person, or not? Do you share the same values and dreams, or not?

If you chose mostly (c) you most likely haven't found your twin flame.

Your answers indicate that you haven't found your twin flame yet. But you might have found a soul mate, soul friend, soul companion, or soul teacher! Take the test in Appendix 2 if you haven't already to determine what kind of relationship you might have.

Thank you for taking this test! You might like to try an interesting experiment with your partner (if you have one) and get them to take it. See what result they get and compare your results!

DID YOU LIKE TWIN FLAMES AND SOUL MATES?

Thank you so much for purchasing *Twin Flames and Soul Mates*. We're honored that you have chosen our book to help you understand your relationship or find a spiritual partnership that meets your soul's needs. We truly hope you've enjoyed this book and now have greater clarity, understanding, and practical advice to apply to your life.

We would like to ask you for a small favor. Would you please take just a minute to leave a review for this book on Amazon or Goodreads? This feedback will help us continue to write the kind of books that will best serve you and others. If you really loved this book, please let us know!

You can also tag us on social media using the hashtag **#twinsoulbook** to let us know your thoughts and feelings about this book!

References

Introduction

1. Twin Flame Community: https://www.facebook.com/groups/TwinFlamesCommunity/

Chapter 1

1. Powell, John. 1974. *The Secret Of Staying In Love.* Allen, TX: Tabor Pub.

Chapter 3

1. Brontë, Emily. *Wuthering Heights.* Harlow: Longman, 1989.

2. Rilke, Rainer Maria, and Reginald Snell. *Letters to a Young Poet.* Mineola, NY: Dover Publications, 2019.

3. Plato, Christopher Gill, and H. D. P. Lee. *The Symposium.* London: Penguin, 2005.

Chapter 5

1. Shadow Work Journal: https://lonerwolf.com/product/shadow-work-journal/

Chapter 7

1. Walsh, Roger, Frances Vaughan, John Welwood, et al. *Paths beyond Ego: Transpersonal Vision*. New York: J.P. Tarcher, 1994.

Chapter 8

1. Dweck, Carol S. 2017. *Mindset*. London: Robinson.

2. Whyte, David. *Consolations: The Solace, Nourishment and Underlying Meaning of Everyday Words*. Langley, WA: Many Rivers Press, 2015.

3. Goldsmith, Neal M. *Psychedelic Healing: The Promise of Entheogens for Psychotherapy and Spiritual Development*. Rochester, VT: Healing Arts Press, 2011.

Chapter 9

1. Nayyirah Waheed poetry: https://www.nayyirahwaheed.com
2. Gibran, Kahlil. *Tear and Smile*. S.l.: Blurb, 2018.
3. Brown, Jeff. *An Uncommon Bond*. Toronto, Canada: Enrealment Press, 2015.

Chapter 10

1. Mistlberger, P. T. *Rude Awakening - Perils, Pitfalls, and Hard Truths of the Spiritual Path.* John Hunt Publishing, 2012.

Chapter 11

1. Mistlberger, P. T. *The Inner Light: Self-realization via the Western Esoteric Tradition.* Alresford, Hants: Axis Mundi Books, 2014.
2. Zukav, Gary. *The Seat of the Soul.* New York: Simon and Schuster, 1989.
3. Nepo, Mark. *The Book of Awakening: Having the Life You Want By Being Present in the Life You Have.* London: Quercus, 2012.

What Next?

1. Barks, Coleman, and Jalāl Ad-Dīn Muhammad Rūmī. *The Essential Rumi.* New York: Castle Books, 1995.

Bibliography

Berne, Eric. *Games People Play: The Psychology of Human Relationships.* London: Penguin Life, 2016.

Bradshaw, John. *Homecoming: Reclaiming and Championing Your Inner Child.* London: Piatkus, 1990.

Burgo, Joseph. *Why Do I Do That?: Psychological Defense Mechanisms and the Hidden Ways They Shape Our Lives.* Chapel Hill, NC: New Rise Press, 2012.

Chapman, Gary D. *The Five Love Languages: How to Express Heartfelt Commitment to Your Mate.* Nashville, TN: LifeWay Press, 2010.

Duhigg, Charles. *The Power of Habit: Why We Do What We Do in Life and Business.* Toronto: Anchor Canada, 2014.

Goleman, Daniel. *Emotional Intelligence: Why It Can Matter More than IQ.* London: Bloomsbury, 2004.

Johnson, Robert A. *Owning Your Own Shadow - Understanding the Dark Side of the Psyche.* Harpercollins Publishers, 1994.

Rosenberg, Marshall B. *Non-violent Communication: A Language of Life.* Encinitas, CA: PuddleDancer Press, 2015.

Tatkin, Stan. *Wired for Love: How Understanding Your Partner's Brain and Attachment Style Can Help You Defuse Conflict and Build a Secure Relationship.* Oakland: New Harbinger, 2012.

About the Authors

Aletheia Luna and Mateo Sol are twin flames and spiritual counselors who united on 11.11.11 and created their popular website *lonerwolf* shortly thereafter. They blend a mixture of psychological and spiritual insight throughout their writings and believe in the value of teaching a down-to-earth approach to spirituality. Their work has been featured and mentioned in respected websites such as The Huffington Post, PsychCentral, and Elephant Journal. To date, they have written over six hundred articles and published numerous books on a variety of spiritual topics.

You can read more of their work and subscribe to their free weekly newsletter on https://lonerwolf.com.

Other Books by the Authors

Awakened Empath

Written for the highly sensitive and empathic people of life, *Awakened Empath* is a comprehensive map for helping all sensitives everywhere to develop physical, mental, emotional, and spiritual balance on every level. Empaths are people who absorb the emotions of others like a sponge and experiences these emotions as their own. In this book, those who struggle with this unique trait are taught how to strengthen, harmonize, and use their gifts to live life to the fullest and awaken as spiritual beings having a human experience.

The Spiritual Awakening Process

Created for those who feel lost and alone in life, *The Spiritual Awakening Process* maps the journey of inner awakening and how to fulfill your personal destiny. With crystal clear and penetrating insight, spiritual mentors Luna and Sol help you to explore how to navigate through this chaotic life period in order to embody your highest calling. This book explores topics such as the dark night of the soul, soul loss, soul retrieval, inner child work, and many other topics which will help you to evolve into the awakened being you're destined to become.

Made in the USA
Columbia, SC
30 January 2021

32021773R00171